CROCHET SHAPES

Quadrille, Penguin Random House UK,
One Embassy Gardens, 8 Viaduct Gardens,
London SW11 7BW

Quadrille Publishing Limited is part of the Penguin Random House group of companies whose addresses can be found at global.penguinrandomhouse.com

Penguin Random House UK

Published by Quadrille in 2025

www.penguin.co.uk

A CIP catalogue record for this book is available from the British Library

ISBN 9781837833573
10 9 8 7 6 5 4 3 2 1

Editorial Director: Harriet Butt
Managing Editor: Chelsea Edwards
Design: Claire Warner Studio
Photographer: Rachel Manns
Photographer's assistants: Merve Prestedge, Abi Hendrie, Suki Simm, Imogen Faulkner and Phoebe Francis
Illustrator: Esther Coombs
Production Manager: Sabeena Atchia
Copy Editor: Lindsay Kaubi
Proofreader: Marie Clayton
Colour reproduction by F1

Printed in China by C&C Offset Printing Co., Ltd.

The authorised representative in the EEA is Penguin Random House Ireland, Morrison Chambers, 32 Nassau Street, Dublin D02 YH68.

FSC
www.fsc.org
MIX
Paper | Supporting responsible forestry
FSC® C018179

Penguin Random House is committed to a sustainable future for our business, our readers and our planet. This book is made from Forest Stewardship Council® certified paper.

15 Projects, 6 Motifs,
Endless Crochet Combinations!

CROCHET SHAPES

KATIE JONES

Quadrille

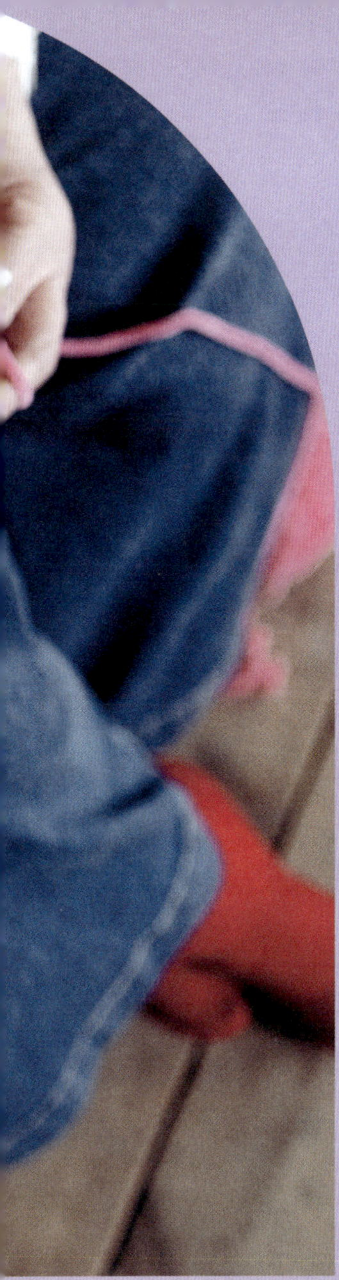

INTRODUCTION 7
ABOUT THIS BOOK 8

GETTING STARTED 10
Glossary of crochet terms 12
US/UK terms 12
Tools 14
Yarns 16
Getting your grip 18
Guide to stitches 20
Tension 27

THE SHAPES 28
Granny Square 32
Half 'n' Half Square 36
Pentagon 42
Hexagon 46
Half Hexi 50
Octagon 54

DESIGN AND MAKE 60
Planning your project and customizing designs 62
Yarn choice 64
Colourways 66
Colour and pattern 68
Calculating your yarn needs 70
Colour techniques 72
Joining techniques 76
Fit, feel and sizing 82
Rows, rounds and ribs 84
Double crochet rows and rounds 86
Granny stitch rows and rounds 88
Rib stitch 90
Finishing 92
Crochet care 94

THE PROJECTS 96
Shape It Up Blanket 98
Beret 104
Cushion Cover 108
Knot Bag 112
Collar 116
Perfect Pouch 120
Neckerchief Scarf 124
Cozy Cowboy Slipper Socks 128
Floor Cushion Cozy 134
Simple Squares Shopper 140
Colour Lovin' Coatigan 144
Bonnet 152
Patchwork Jumper 156
Tabard 162
Vest 168

About the Author 174
Suppliers 176
Thanks 176

CONTENTS

INTRODUCTION

Join me in the colourful crafted world of crochet shapes and move beyond the square!

Get your granny on and move beyond the square! Come and join me in the colourful crafted world of crochet shapes.

The granny square, a timeless classic, has captivated crocheters for generations and it's where my personal obsession with crochet began! It is a simple yet versatile design, which has made it a firm favourite for blankets, garments, and accessories. I love it so much that my first book was all about the square, but why stop there? Don't limit yourself to squares, let's use our granny stitch technique and explore a variety of shapes! A traditional granny square is characterised by clusters of three treble stitches worked in a square formation. This 'granny' cluster, a fundamental building block, can be adapted to create a range of shapes beyond the square. In this book we will also be exploring pentagons, hexagons and octagons, too.

One of crochet's biggest selling points is the ability to build designs from smaller motifs; this means you can break projects down into bite-sized chunks. As well as making bigger projects more accessible by breaking them down into smaller parts, it also means it's great for taking pieces around with you to complete on the go. Making it the perfect portable craft! For me, this is why I love motif work so much, because from a smaller simple piece you can make amazing more complex designs.

The 'granny square' is the ultimate classic crochet motif, which first appeared in print in *The Art of Crocheting* in 1891. Its name is thought to derive from its clear, defined pattern, which could be easily felt, making it accessible to those with limited vision, particularly Grannies. A big part of its popularity is due to the ability to feel out the pattern; once you get the hang of it, you don't have to look at your work all the time when crocheting, making it the perfect stitch to do whilst chatting, on the go or sat on the sofa with your favourite box set!

The crochet motif has undeniably captured the hearts of crocheters worldwide, with the granny stitch holding a special place in my heart because I inherited my love for crochet from my own Granny, who had a colourful blanket for every surface. I have taken this as my inspiration in life and during my time as a crochet designer I have tried to cover as much as I can in colourful crochet, too!

For the last decade I have worked as a crochet designer, and have my own brand developed with the help of my mum, Annie. The granny stitch has reigned supreme and been prevalent in my work: some of my highlights have to be filling a Selfridges Oxford Street window with colourful granny goodness and having my designs in a V&A exhibition! I LOVE covering as much as I can in colourful crochet (including myself), but my real passion is sharing my love for crochet and helping to get you hooked, too!

ABOUT THIS BOOK

Whether you're a seasoned crocheter or a curious beginner, this book is your ultimate guide to creating stunning projects out of a range of fun shapes.

I'll take you on a journey through six essential crochet shapes: the Square, Half 'n' Half Square, Pentagon, Hexagon, Half Hexi and Octagon. There are also 15 inspiring designs to make with the shapes for you and your home. These patterns are just the starting point! Follow along with my examples or mix and match colours and yarns to create your own unique designs; from cosy blankets to stylish accessories and garments, the possibilities are endless!

This crochet handbook is packed with step-by-step instructions, photos to inspire and illustrations to help you master each technique. I will be using UK crochet terms for the patterns (but we also have a conversion table for US terms) and instructions are written in longhand format to take you through each step as if I were in the room with you talking through each part. As an added extra, to accompany the book, you can also scan the QR code on each shape motif page to find a handy step-by-step video to guide you through the making process.

Treat this book as more than just a collection of patterns; it's a creative companion that will inspire you to experiment, learn new techniques, push the boundaries of your imagination and create custom pieces that you'll cherish for years to come.

So, grab your hook, pick a pattern and let's embark on a crafty colourful creative adventure together!

GETTING STARTED

GLOSSARY OF CROCHET TERMS

When you start crocheting it might feel like reading a foreign language, and that's because it really is! It has a whole vocabulary of its own, and its own regional dialects!

There are two main types of crochet term used, UK and US, and though most of the same stitch names are used in UK and US terminology, the stitch that you're working is different. This can catch you out in the beginning and be a bit confusing, but once you get to grips with it you will become fluent. This book is written using UK terms and I have included a conversion chart for the US equivalents. In this section, we will break down the terms and their meanings. I have included the stitch abbreviations for reference here; however, all patterns in this book are written in longhand to make the steps as easy to follow as possible.

Alongside the motifs' written instructions you will also find schematic drawings. I LOVE crochet charts because they are universal, so these are a really helpful reference and if you are a more visual learner, you may find these easier to follow.

Stitches, Abbreviations and Terms

UK TERMS		SYMBOL	US TERMS	
Stitch	St		Stitch	St
Chain	CH		Chain	CH
Slip stitch	Sl St	•	Slip stitch	Sl St
Double crochet	DC	+	Single crochet	SC
Half treble	HTR		Half double crochet	HDC
Treble	TR		Double crochet	DC
Cluster (treble 3)	CL		Cluster (double crochet 3)	CL
Double treble	DTR		Treble	TR
Treble 2 together	TR2TOG		Double crochet 2 together	DC2TOG

ADDING IN YARN
Sometimes when crocheting you will run out of yarn, or your yarn will have a join mid row/round. This means you will need to join in a new strand of yarn. If your yarn has a knot in it that you do not trust to hold (I never trust them), snip out the knot. Leave at least 8cm (3⅛in) of your existing yarn to sew in and an 8cm (3⅛in) tail of your new yarn and either pinch these together and work the next stitch or tie with a knot. You can then either work over the ends or sew them in to secure.

BLOCK/BLOCKING
Flattening and neatening crochet motifs/fabric once completed by pinning out and dampening or steaming them to shape and leaving to dry.

BORDER
Edging crochet motifs or finished pieces to extend, decorate or neaten the work.

BRACKETS (...)
Stitches shown together in brackets are to be worked into the same stitch or space.

CHAIN SPACE
A series of chain stitches creating a space between two stitches.

CHANGING COLOUR
I like to secure my yarn when changing colour: fasten off the old colour and join in the new colour with a slip stitch. If you're changing colours when working the motifs in this book, start the new colour in a different corner each time to spread out your yarn ends. This will prevent one section of your design feeling bulky when you sew in the yarn tails at the end.

CLUSTER(S)
There's no fixed definition for this term because it's used differently to abbreviate a grouping of stitches. In this book, a cluster refers to a group of three treble crochets worked into the same stitch or gap.

CROCHET IN YARN ENDS
On some motifs it is possible to crochet over yarn ends as the work progresses. This reduces the number of ends to be woven in when the project is completed.

DECREASE
Reducing the number of stitches by working several stitches together.

EASE
Ease is the difference between the measurements of the garment and the measurements of the intended wearer.

FASTEN OFF
Finishing off the last stitch securely so that it stops the work from unravelling.

FOUNDATION CHAIN
A foundation chain is a length of chain which starts a project off.

FOUNDATION RING
The first set of chain stitches, which when joined together, form the base for the first round of crochet.

INCREASE
Increasing the number of stitches by working more than one stitch in the same place.

RIGHT SIDE
The side of the crochet that will be on show once completed.

ROUND
A series of crochet stitches worked around a central starting point, or piece edge, and joined together in the place where you started.

ROW
A series of crochet stitches worked along an edge, working back and forth.

SCHEMATIC CHART
A chart comprised of symbols representing stitches to illustrate a pattern. Use the stitch key in the Stitches, Abbreviations and Terms chart for reference. To read a schematic, follow the diagram working from the centre outwards, round by round. The schematics are designed for right-handed working, which is followed by reading anticlockwise. If you are left-handed you should follow the stitches in a clockwise direction.

SLIP KNOT
The knot used to create the loop on the crochet hook that acts as the first chain.

SPACE
The gap between stitches.

TENSION (GAUGE)
The number of stitches and rows made over a set measurement. For garments it will be important to achieve the correct size, for blankets the correct tension may not be so vital.

TOTAL STITCHES
Can refer to a stitch of any size. Used to show total number of stitches in a round or row in brackets on pattern instructions.

TURN
Reverse the motif/fabric to work with the other side facing you.

WEAVE IN ENDS
After fastening off, weave any ends of yarn into the motif/main fabric so they cannot be seen. This can be done with a yarn needle or latch tool, and it is recommended that you weave in as you complete each motif to save having a huge task at the end.

WORKING INTO THE BACK OF THE STITCH
Working a stitch into the back top strand of stitch (single strand).

WORKING INTO THE STITCH
Working a stitch into the top of the stitch under the two top strands.

WORKING INTO THE SPACE/GAP
Working into the space or gap between the stitches.

WRONG SIDE
The side of the motif/fabric which will not be seen when the item is completed.

YARN ROUND HOOK
Wind the yarn around the hook from back to front, anticlockwise.

KATIE JONES

TOOLS

One of the amazing things about crochet is that you need very little equipment; all you need to get started is a hook and some yarn. Crochet is super portable, so it's perfect for the sofa, public transport or even a day at the beach! The following tools are recommended for the projects:

The Essentials

HOOKS
Hooks can be made from several materials including metal, bamboo, plastic and wood. They can have straight handles or shaped plastic grips, which some people find more comfortable to hold. The type of hook you use is a matter of personal choice and you may have to try a few different types before you find the one you feel happiest with.

Hooks come in many sizes from a 2mm to 10mm or even larger, going up in half sizes (2.5mm, 3mm, 3.5mm etc.) The size of the hook is usually stamped on the handle. Most crochet in DK, Aran or chunky weight yarn is done on hook sizes ranging from 3mm to 7mm. It is preferable to store all your hooks together in a roll or small bag as they can easily get lost.

STITCH MARKERS
These are usually made of brightly coloured plastic or metal and shaped like small safety pins. They are used to mark specific places in stitch patterns or rows.

TAPE MEASURE
Useful for measuring pattern sizing, checking crochet tension and for checking the size of motifs and finished garments

SMALL SCISSORS/YARN NIPPERS
To cut yarn cleanly and snip yarn ends after weaving in.

YARN/TAPESTRY NEEDLES
Large-eyed plastic or metal needles, which are used to sew crochet together and weave in yarn ends.

NOTEBOOK/SQUARED PAPER
To note any changes to a pattern (e.g., different hook size used) and draw out your designs

CALCULATOR
To calculate the amount of yarn required for the finished piece.

Other Useful Equipment

LARGE-HEADED PINS
For use when blocking out motifs or garments.

STEAM IRON/WATER SPRAY
For dampening the motifs or garments when blocking.

IRONING BOARD/CHILDREN'S FOAM PLAY MAT
For pinning out motifs and garments when blocking.

CRAYONS/COLOURED PENS
To plan the colours to be used in your pieces.

LATCH HOOK
A latch hook is a piece of equipment that can be used as an alternative to a needle for weaving in ends.

PROJECT BAG
To keep your hooks and yarn together.

DIGITAL SCALES (KITCHEN SCALES)
To calculate the amount of yarn needed for each piece by weighing a motif and multiplying the results. Especially useful if using a different yarn weight for one of the patterns, or if you are using yarn scraps to make projects.

YARN

Yarn is a general term for a strand of textile fibres spun together. It comes in a huge range of textures fibres, colours and weights. With so many different yarns out there, it can be hard to know where to start!

Yarn can be made from natural source materials like wool or cotton, synthetic materials like acrylic, or even recycled materials. Each type of yarn has its own unique properties, which will affect the final look and feel of your project.

The table below shows all the different yarn weights with their recommended hook size ranges. The information on what yarn type and recommended hook to use is also often printed on the yarn label. Sometimes the label may only have the knitting needle size, don't worry, you can also use this as a rough guide for your hook.

2 FINE	3 LIGHT	4 MEDIUM	5 BULKY	6 SUPER BULKY 7 JUMBO
Baby Sport 2/3/4 ply	Double knit DK	Aran Worsted	Chunky	Super chunky Jumbo
Hooks 2.5–3.5 mm	Hooks 3–4.5 mm	Hooks 4.5–6.5 mm	Hooks 6–9 mm	Hooks 9–20mm

A yarn store is like a sweet shop for crocheters! You can feel the different textures, see the colours and be inspired. It's a great way to understand how different yarns feel, especially if you're making something you'll wear. There are some fab online shops, but nothing beats visiting your local yarn store and seeing that yarn in person!

Natural fibres like cotton and wool are popular; they are breathable and have a more circular lifecycle, while synthetic fibres like acrylic offer durability and affordability – these are especially good for larger projects like blankets. You will also find blends that combine the best of both worlds, a cotton blend is one of my favourites to use for feel, wear, great colours and easy washability. Some yarns are better suited to certain seasons. Wools and fluffy fibres are perfect for keeping warm in the colder months, while cotton is ideal for keeping cooler in warmer weather.

In this book, we've chosen yarns in easy-to-find, popular weights. We've provided the weight and tension information for each project, but you have the freedom to choose your own colours, brands and fibre types. Let your creativity shine! More details on the brands used to produce the sample projects in this book can be found on page 176.

Yarn is typically sold by weight, not length. This means that no two balls of the same yarn weight are the same and can have slightly different lengths, depending on the brand and specific yarn. To help you estimate yarn usage, our patterns provide meterage information. This gives you a rough idea of how much yarn you'll need for each project no matter what brand you are using. You can find the meterage information on the yarn ball band. Keep in mind that your personal, actual yarn usage for projects may vary, depending on your tension and the specific yarn you choose.

GETTING YOUR GRIP

Getting a good grip on your hook and yarn can be tricky at first, but don't be discouraged it just takes a bit of practice!

Most of us aren't used to being so dexterous with both hands, so holding your hook and yarn can feel awkward at first, but with patience and persistence, you'll soon develop the muscle memory needed to hold them comfortably. The key is to find a grip that feels natural to you and allows you to maintain consistent tension.

PENCIL HOLD

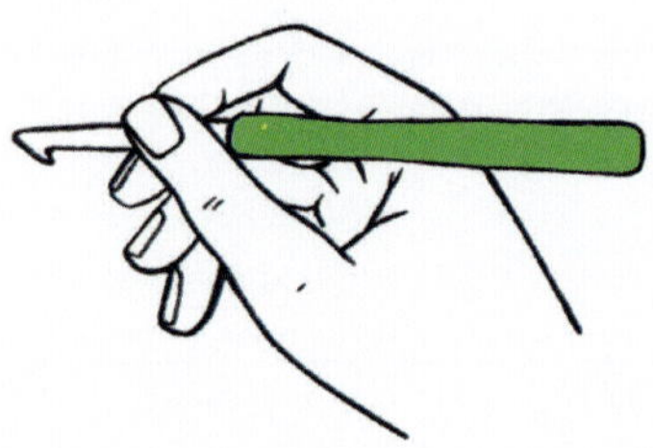

KNIFE HOLD

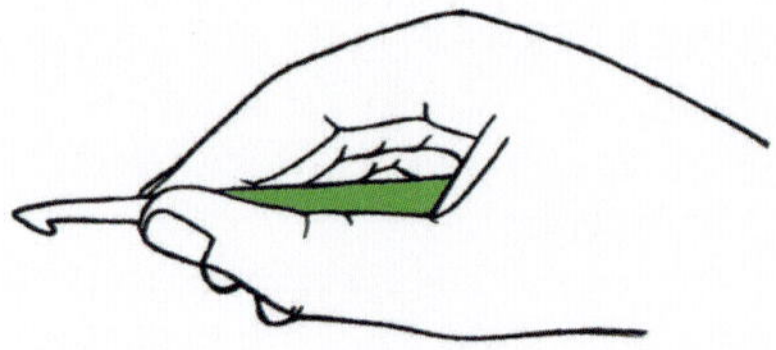

If you're new to crochet, the best way to get started is by practising the chain stitch. I know it's tempting to jump right into a bigger project but starting small by training your hands can really help you build the skills you need to make that first project 'chef's kiss' perfect. Put on your favorite tunes and keep chaining until it becomes second nature. You'll be amazed at how quickly your hands will start to remember the motions. Trust me, practice really does make perfect!

Holding the Hook

Rule number one is there are no fixed rules! There is no right or wrong way to hold your hook. You should hold the hook in your dominant hand, and it needs to feel comfortable to you. Shown left are the two most popular ways to hold the hook.

Holding the Yarn

Your non-dominant hand does – what I think – is all the hard work in crochet and getting your yarn hold right and feeling comfortable can take time. There are no set rules, but finding a way to keep your tension smooth is really important. My top tip is to try to hold your hand in such a way that you have an 'antenna' finger because this helps with keeping smooth tension. My personal favorite hold is the 'shadow puppet bunny'. This may sound silly but it's a good way to remember the hand positioning.

Getting your yarn grip sorted will help the smoothness of stitching and the flow of your work. Grab your hook and some yarn to match its size, starting off with a chunkier yarn will really help in mastering your hand hold before trying new stitches.

Shadow Puppet Bunny

1 To set your hand up in this formation, either loop the yarn around your little finger or pinch it there to help keep tension.

2 The yarn then loops from the inside of your hand over the top of your fingers.

3 Hold your hand in a shadow puppet bunny shape using either your thumb and forefinger or middle finger (bunny mouth). Where your fingers meet, pinch the yarn and hold the working yarn close to the hook. Your middle finger or forefinger (the bunny ear) then works as your 'antenna', maintaining an area of smooth, taut yarn for tension.

4 This area between your pinch and 'antenna' is where you hook the yarn to create the stitch. By circling your hook and working over the yarn in this area, the yarn catches on the hook and is easy to pull through as a stitch without dropping off.

RIGHT-HANDED GRIP

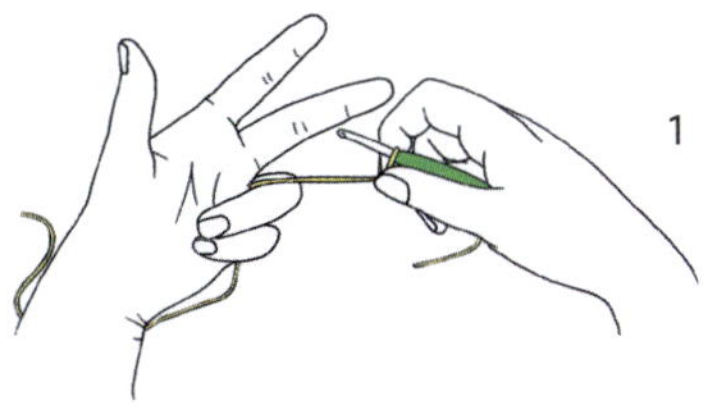

1

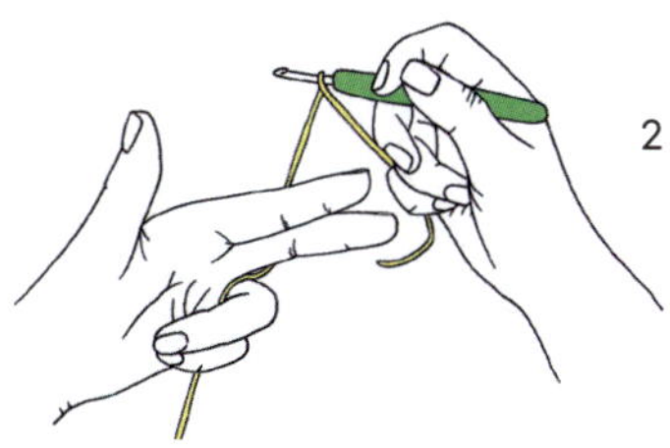

2

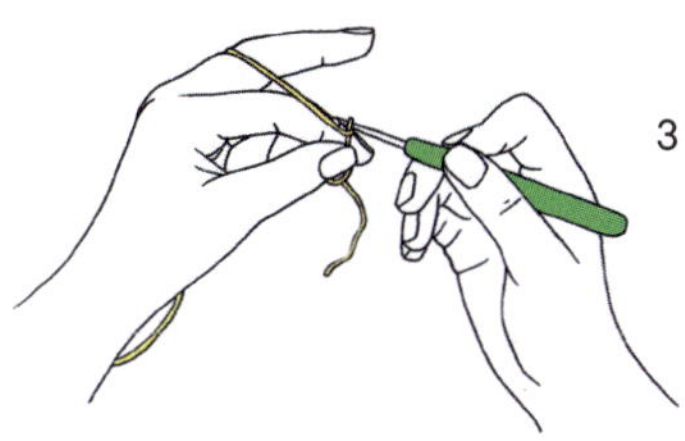

3

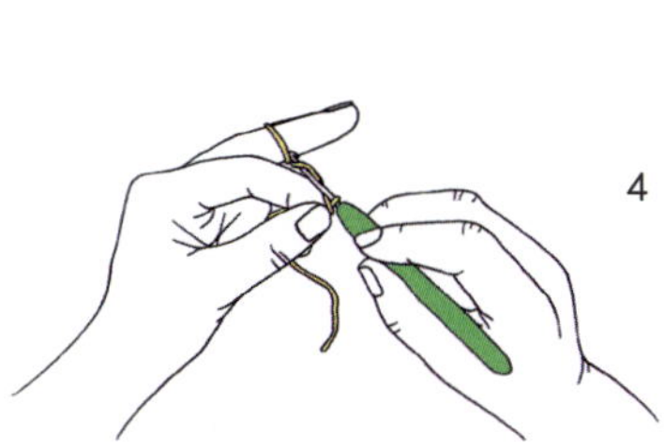

4

LEFT-HANDED GRIP

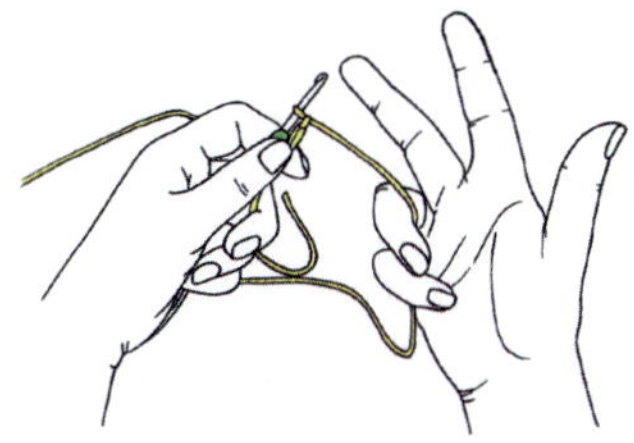

1

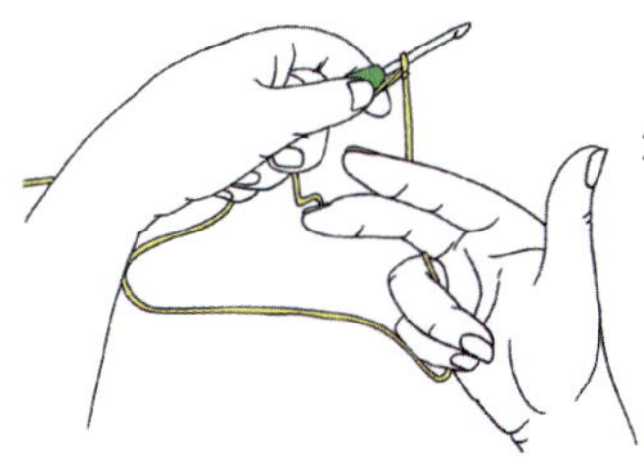

2

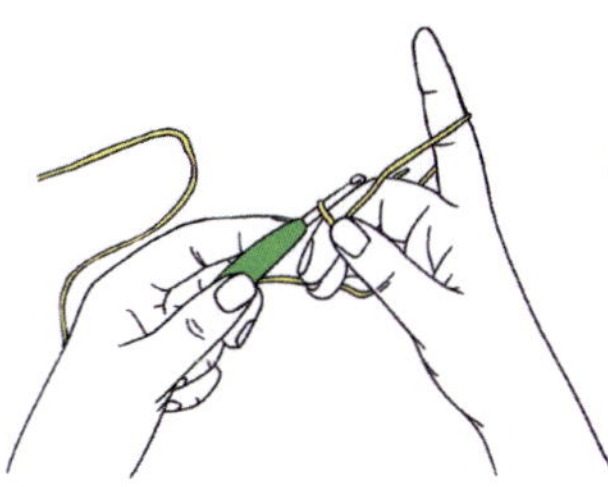

3

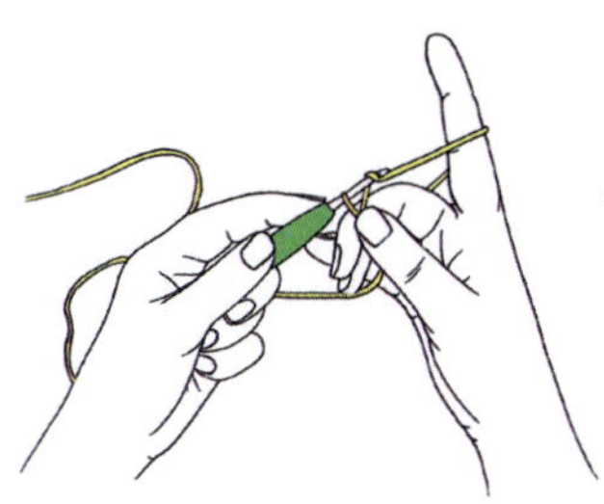

4

GUIDE TO STITCHES

Now you know how to hold your yarn and hook, let's get to know all the basic stitches!

This illustrated guide takes you step by step through all the stitches you will need to whip up your shape motifs and projects. Just remember, the stitch guide and patterns in this book are given in UK crochet terms.

If you are new to crochet, I recommend grabbing a hook and some yarn and giving some of these stitches a go before starting your first project!

Slip Knot

This is the knot that becomes the first loop on your hook, this knot is not counted as a stitch. When starting you should leave a yarn tail that is long enough to weave in at the end.

1 Make a loop with the yarn. Insert the hook through the middle of the loop, hook the yarn and pull it through.

2 This is your slip knot. The loop is adjustable, pull it so that it is snug but not too tight, against the hook.

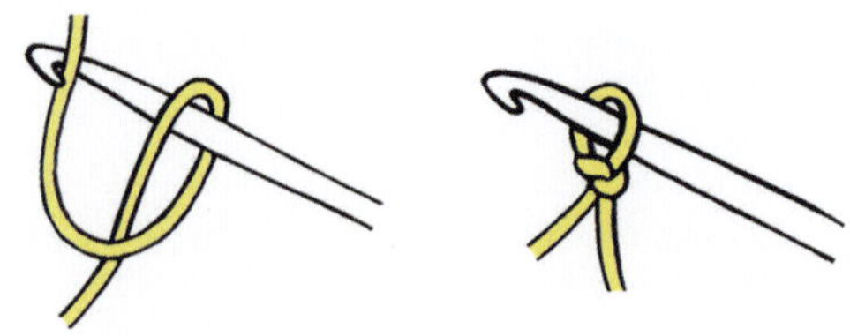

1 2

Chain Stitch

This is a single stitch that can be worked consecutively to form a chain. All stitches start with the slip knot on the hook.

1 To begin your first chain, wrap the yarn around the hook anticlockwise (clockwise if left-handed).

2 Catch the yarn with the hook and pull the yarn through the slip knot on the hook.

3 This is your first chain stitch – only when a stitch is off the hook does it count as a stitch. Make the next chain by wrapping the yarn around the hook and pulling it through the loop on the hook again. Continue to produce the required number of chain stitches.

4 As you work, hold the chain being created with your non-dominant hand near the hook to control the tension. You will need to reposition your hand every few stitches to ensure you keep an even tension.

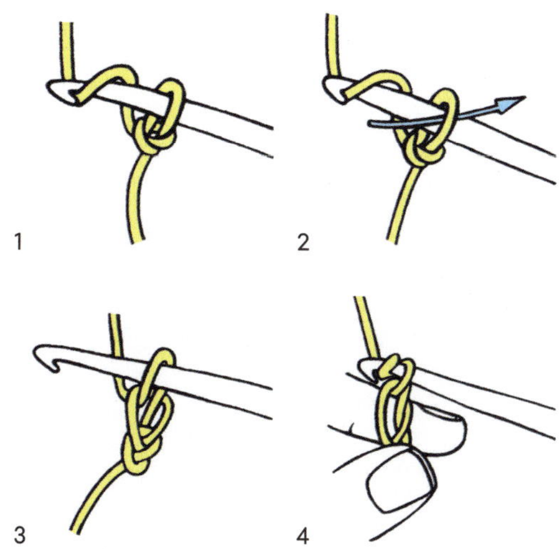

Anatomy of a Chain

A crochet chain has a front and back. The front looks like a series of 'v' shapes, on the back is a series of bumps. Each v shape or bump equals one chain.

FRONT OF CHAIN

BACK OF CHAIN

Slip Stitch

Slip stitches have no height and are used as joining stitches and in places where you need to move along a row or round.

1 Insert the hook into the next stitch.

2 Wrap the yarn around the hook and pull it through not only the stitch but also the first loop on the hook.

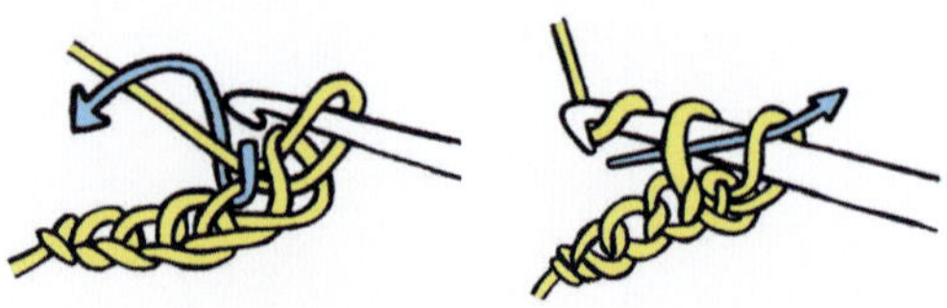

1 2

Foundation Ring

This method forms a ring into which you can begin crocheting your first round.

1 Make a chain with the number of stitches specified in the pattern.

2 Close the ring by inserting the hook into the first chain and working a slip stitch by pulling the yarn through both loops.

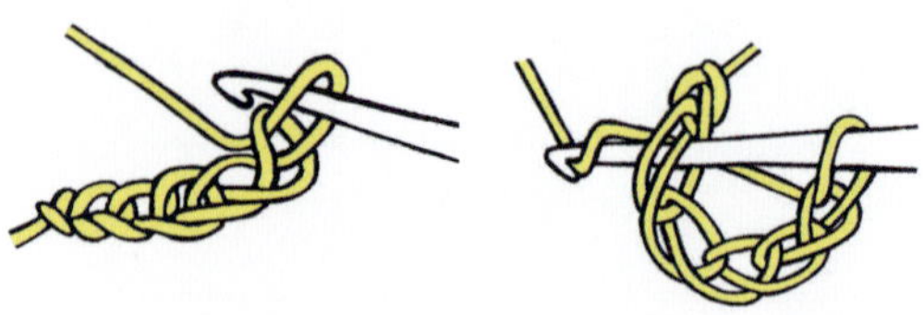

1 2

Double Crochet

Double crochet stitches are simple, compact stitches that form a dense fabric and are often used in edgings and toy making. They can also be used for joining two pieces of fabric (see page 81).

1. Insert the hook into the stitch or space. Wrap the yarn around hook and pull the yarn through to the front.
2. You should have two loops on your hook. Wrap the yarn around the hook.
3. Pull the yarn through both loops. There should be one loop left on your hook. You have created a double crochet.

1

2

3

Half Treble

A stitch that's halfway between a double crochet and a treble in height and looks slightly looser than a double crochet. Often used when shaping edges and in motifs.

1. Wrap the yarn around hook and insert the hook into the stitch or space. Wrap the yarn around hook and pull the yarn through to the front.
2. You should now have three loops on your hook. Wrap the yarn around the hook and pull through all three loops, leaving one loop on your hook.
3. You have created a half treble crochet.

1

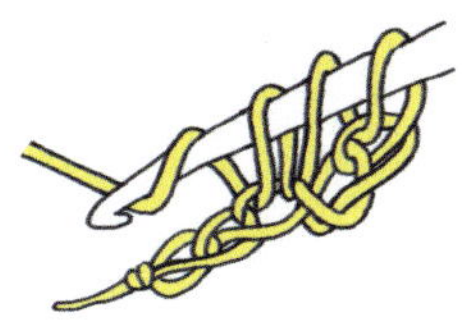

2

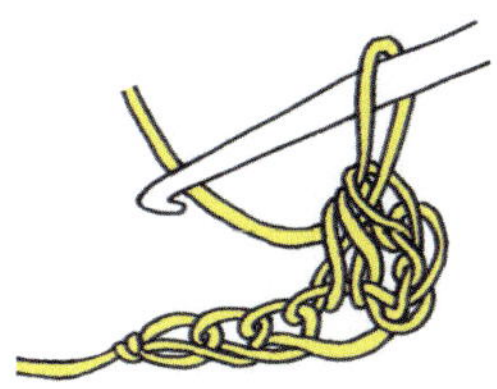

3

Treble Crochet

This is probably the most popular crochet stitch for use in granny squares. It is twice the height of a double crochet stitch.

1 Wrap the yarn around the hook and insert the hook into the stitch or space. Wrap the yarn round hook and pull the yarn through to the front.

2 You should have three loops on your hook. Wrap the yarn around the hook and pull through two loops.

3 You should have two loops on your hook. Wrap the yarn around the hook and pull through the final two loops, leaving one loop on your hook.

4 You have created a treble crochet.

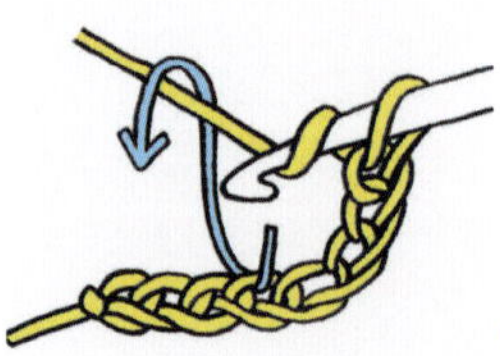

1

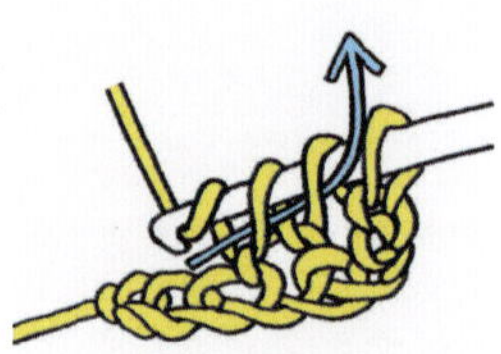

2

3

4

Double Treble Crochet

This is worked in the same way as a treble crochet stitch, but the yarn is wrapped around the hook twice to start.

1 Wrap the yarn around the hook twice. Insert the hook into the stitch or space. Wrap the yarn round hook and pull the yarn through to the front.

2 You should have four loops on your hook. Wrap the yarn around the hook and pull the yarn through the first two loops.

3 You should have three loops on your hook. Wrap the yarn around the hook and pull the yarn through the next two loops.

4 Two loops on your hook. Wrap the yarn around the hook and pull it through the final two loops.

5 One loop left on the hook. This completes the double treble crochet.

1

2

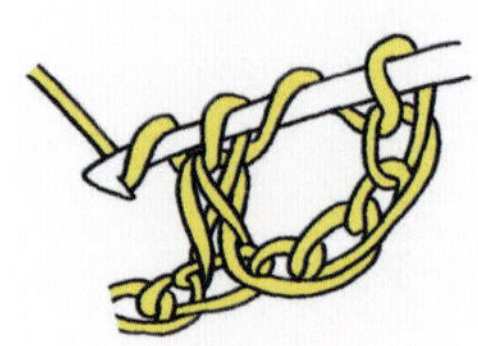

3

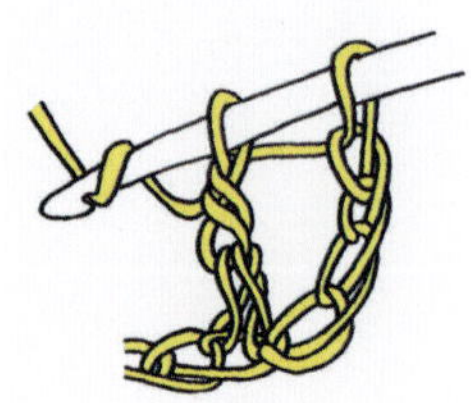

4

5

Working into the back of the chain

This technique is used to create cords or ties with a neat edge by working into the back bump of the chain. The technique is used with slip stitches or double crochets in this book and means each side of the work will have the V-plait style edging.

1 Chain for amount given in pattern.

2 Following the stitch type given in the pattern, work into the back bump of the chain.

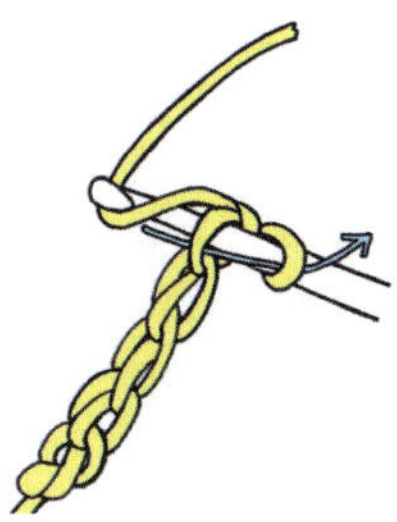

1

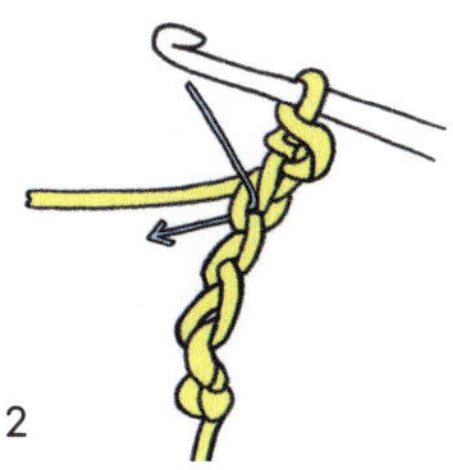

2

3

Double Crocheting or Trebling Together

This technique involves working trebles or double crochets together and is done by working the last but one step of the stitch, but instead of pulling through the final two loops you begin the next stitch. Repeat this process for the number and type of stitches given in the pattern, and then pull the yarn through all the loops on your hook for the final step. This is one way to reduce the number of stitches.

WORKING IN DIFFERENT STITCHES TO REDUCE/DECREASE

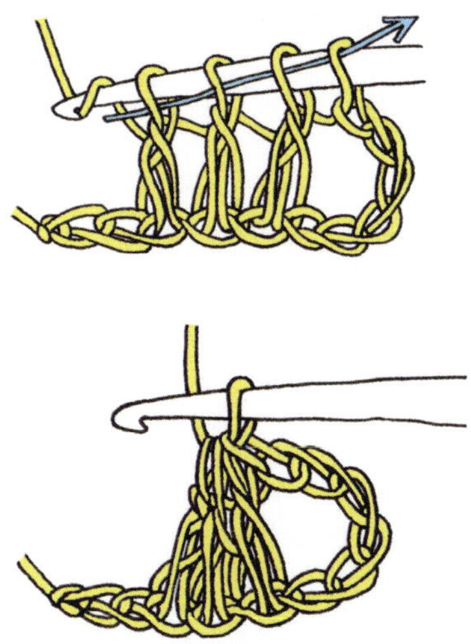

Working Stitches into a Foundation Ring

The square motifs in this book all start with a foundation ring and the stitches of the first round are worked by inserting the hook into the centre of the ring. Turning chains are used to get to the right height for the stitches of your first round. If you work over the yarn tail as you stitch into the foundation ring for the first round, you can pull the tail to close up your central hole – if you wish to.

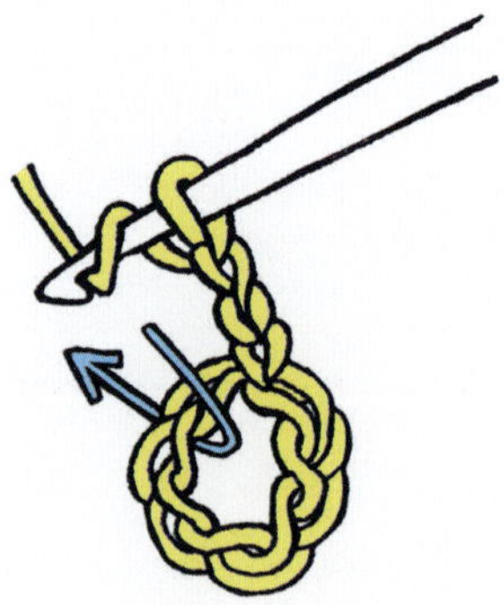

Turning Chains

If you're crocheting in rows or rounds you will need to add turning chains at the beginning of each row/round. This acts as a fake first stitch of the row/round and is used to bring the hook up to the height of the stitches you are crocheting. Each basic stitch has its own number of chains. For double crochet this is 1 chain, for half trebles 2 chains, for trebles 3 chains and for double trebles 4 chains. If you want to count the total number of stitches in a row or round, remember to include your turning chain fake stitch in this.

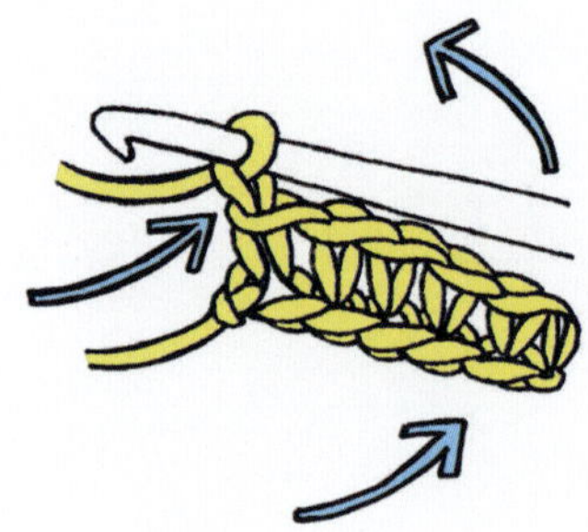

Fastening Off

Finish with a slip stitch join or final stitch.

1 Make one chain.

2 Cut the yarn, leaving a yarn tail at least 8–10cm (3⅛–4in) long (or more if specified in the pattern).

3 Pull the cut yarn through the loop of the chain and pull tightly so that the fabric does not unravel.

TENSION

Tension, tension, tension! It's a pretty big deal in crochet. Getting the hang of tension is super important – I think it may even be the most important aspect of getting your makes to look amazing!

Tension refers to how tightly or loosely you crochet and it's measured by counting the number of stitches and rows in a specific area. Things like hook size and yarn weight can affect tension, but because crochet involves pulling yarn through stitches with a hook, your personal style, mood, and even the way you hold your hook and yarn can affect how tightly or loosely you work. When it comes to tension, we are all individuals and this can lead to variations in tension between different crocheters, even when using the same materials and techniques.

Practice, Practice, Practice

If you're a crochet newbie, practice makes perfect! Chain away until your fingers fly. It might feel a bit boring, but trust me, it's worth it. Put on your favourite film or blast your most loved music and spend some time practising the chain stitch to develop that steady rhythm, this will help you achieve even stitches and consistent tension. The more you practise, the better your tension will become. You'll develop a feel for the right amount of grip and pull to apply to your hook and yarn, and before you know it, you'll be crocheting like a pro!

Once you've got your crochet rhythm down, you can start matching your hook size and yarn weight to the pattern's recommended tension. This will help you achieve the desired size for your crochet shapes. All the projects in this book are made from motifs and the tension guide for each project is given by measuring across the shape, flat edge to flat edge. So, when working out your tension start with the recommended hook size for the yarn and see if you can match the tension. If your numbers don't match up, don't worry, tension can really vary from person to person, just remember, it's a lot easier to change your hook size than to try and change yourself. If your crochet comes out too small, try going up a hook size and if your tension is coming out too large, try sizing down.

Make a Tension Swatch

Making a tension swatch is a total game-changer, especially for garments. Even tiny differences in your motif sizes can add up big time when put together in a garment – and no one wants to go and put on their final make to find out it is miles too big or super-duper small! So, grab your hook and yarn and whip up a little swatch. It's not a waste of time I promise you!

For homeware and accessories, like blankets and bags, exact sizing isn't as crucial but will affect the look and feel of a project, and understanding your tension will help you calculate how much yarn you need. Having different tension from the pattern will also affect the yarn usage and meterage calculations given – just keep this in mind if working to a different tension that you may require more yarn.

THE SHAPES

INTRODUCING OUR SIX SHAPES!

1

2

3

4

5

6

1 SQUARE
2 HALF 'N' HALF SQUARE
3 PENTAGON
4 HEXAGON
5 HALF HEXI
6 OCTAGON

Before starting a main project, I recommend making a whole bunch of different shapes.

It's a fun way to practise your stitches, experiment with colours and see how the different motifs look and feel. Grab your hook and yarn and start practising. Refer to the stitch guide on pages 20–26 for detailed instructions.

In the pattern instructions for all the shapes worked in rounds, the yarn colour is changed for each round. Changing colours every round is a great way to see your progress and work on your stitches. For our half shapes worked in rows, it's easier to first practise all in one colour. Once you're comfortable, you can experiment with different colour combinations and create unique patterns. You might prefer to work with one colour for several rounds or switch colours more frequently. The choice is yours!

Granny Square

Say hello to the traditional granny square! This is where my love of the crochet square started and is our first motif! This pattern is worked over four rounds with the stitches worked into the gaps. The granny square is a timeless classic and the most famous of all the squares. Its repeating rounds also make it an easy design to extend into a larger motif.

TOP TIPS

WORKING IN ONE COLOUR

To work the granny square, or any continuing rounds, in the same colour replace steps A, B and C of rounds 2, 3 and 4 with: Slip stitch into the next chain space, chain 5. Continue following the rest of the instructions for the round, omit fastening off if you wish to continue in the same colour.

INCREASING THE SIZE OF YOUR SQUARE

To increase the size of your square, simply repeat round 4, replacing steps E and H with: Work 1 cluster into each gap up to the corner chain space.

Scan to view 'how to' video.

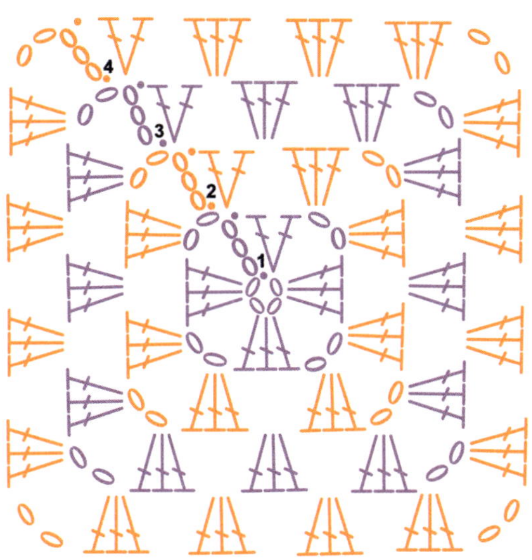

GRANNY SQUARE PATTERN

FOUNDATION

A Using your first colour, chain 4 stitches.
B Slip stitch into the first chain to form your foundation ring.

ROUND 1

A To begin your first round, chain 5 stitches. The first 3 chains count as a fake treble and the next 2 are the first corner. You need chains at the start to get the right stitch height at the centre of your work.
B Work 3 trebles into the centre of the ring.
C (Chain 2, treble 3) into the ring twice to complete your first round.
D Chain 2, treble 2, join with a slip stitch into the third chain at the start of the round to complete the round. The first chain creates the fake treble and the final 2 trebles form the final cluster. From this point on 3 trebles will be known as 1 cluster.
E To fasten off your round, create an extra chain, cut your yarn leaving a tail least 8–10 cm (3⅛–4in) long and pull through the loop to secure.

ROUND 2

A Start with the next colour on your hook.
B Join in with a slip stitch at any chain space. Joining in new colours at different corners for each new round helps distribute where the loose yarn ends are in your squares, and this helps with sewing the ends in neatly when finishing a square.
C Chain 5 stitches.
D Work your first cluster into the same space where you joined in.
E (Cluster, chain 2, cluster) in the following three corner chain spaces.
F Treble 2 into the first chain space.
G Join with a slip stitch into the third chain at the start of the round to complete the round.
H Fasten off.

ROUND 3

A Start with the next colour on your hook.
B Join in with a slip stitch at any chain space.
C Chain 5 stitches.
D Work your first cluster into the same space where you joined in.
E Working into the space between clusters, work 1 cluster.
F (Cluster, chain 2, cluster) into the corner chain space.
G Repeat steps E and F twice more.
H Work 1 cluster into the space.
I Treble 2 into the first chain space.
J Join with a slip stitch into the third chain at the start of the round to complete the round.
K Fasten off.

ROUND 4

A Start with the next colour on your hook.
B Join in with a slip stitch at any corner chain space.
C Chain 5 stitches.
D Work your first cluster into the same space where you joined in.
E Work clusters into the next 2 spaces between clusters.
F (Cluster, chain 2, cluster) into the corner chain space.
G Repeat steps E and F twice more.
H Work clusters into the next 2 spaces between clusters.
I Treble 2 into the first chain space.
J Join with a slip stitch into the third chain at the start of the round to complete the round.
K Fasten off.

Half 'n' Half Square

The half 'n' half square is a graphic take on the classic granny square, where the square is made in two sections – the second side is attached as you work it. Because this motif is made in two halves you can also just use side 1 to create a granny triangle, so it's two shapes for the price of one! This shape is worked in rows, rather than rounds, which means it's worked backwards and forwards, turning to the opposite side at the end of a row, rather than just working on the front of the work.

TOP TIPS

WORKING ROWS IN DIFFERENT COLOURS

See the technique on page 75 for how to change the colour on every row.

CORNERS

The corners of this square aren't all the same, so you'll need to take this into account when joining. For the corners where the two halves meet, work any stitches meant for the corner between the two sides, over the double crochet join.

Scan to view 'how to' video.

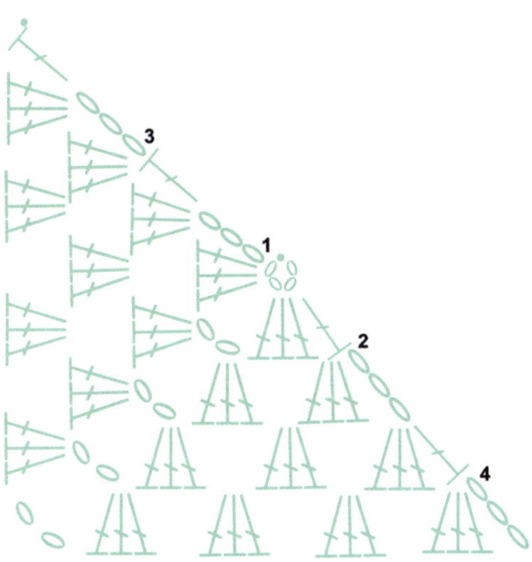

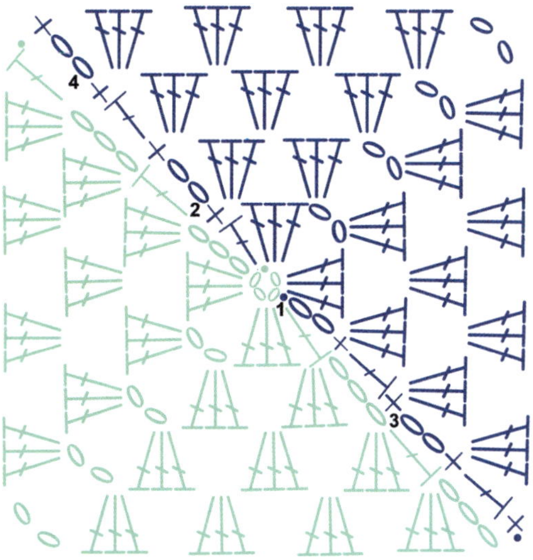

HALF 'N' HALF SQUARE PATTERN

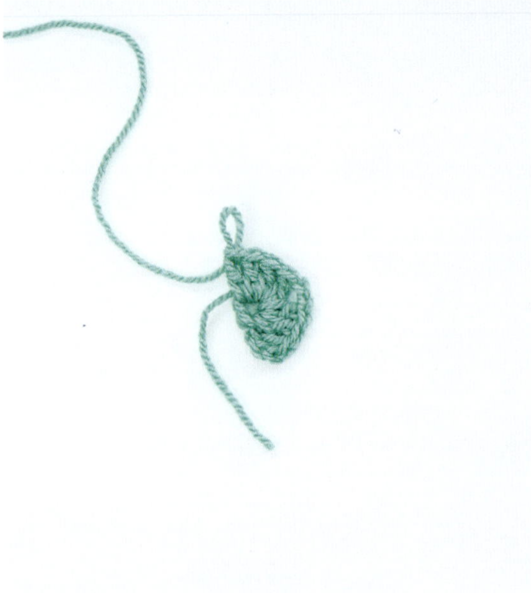

SIDE 1 (WORKED IN FIRST COLOUR)

FOUNDATION

A Using your first colour, chain 4 stitches.
B Slip stitch into the first chain to form your foundation ring.

ROW 1

A To begin the first row, chain 3 stitches. The first 3 chains count as a fake treble. You need chains at the start to get the right stitch height at the centre of your work.
B Work 3 trebles into the centre of the ring. From this point on, 3 trebles will be known as 1 cluster.
C (Chain 2, treble 4) into the ring to complete the first row.
D Turn work.

ROW 2

A Chain 3 stitches.
B Work your first cluster of 3 trebles in the space between the first 2 stitches.
C Miss the next 3 trebles and work (cluster, chain 2, cluster) in the corner chain space.
D Work 1 cluster into the space between the last 2 stitches.
E Treble 1 into the third chain of row 1.
F Turn.

ROW 3

A Chain 3 stitches.
B Work your first cluster between the first 2 stitches.
C Working into the space between clusters, work 1 cluster.
D (Cluster, chain 2, cluster) into the corner chain space.
E Working into the space between clusters, work 1 cluster.
F Work 1 cluster into the space between the last 2 stitches.
G Treble 1 into the third chain of row 2.
H Turn.

ROW 4

A Chain 3 stitches.
B Work your first cluster between the first 2 stitches.
C Work clusters into the next 2 spaces between clusters.
D (Cluster, chain 2, cluster) into the corner chain space.
E Work clusters into the next 2 spaces between clusters.
F Work 1 cluster into the space between the last 2 stitches.
G Treble 1 into the third chain of row 2.
H Fasten off.

Continues overleaf

HALF 'N' HALF GRANNY SQUARE PATTERN

SIDE 2 (WORKED IN SECOND COLOUR)

ROW 1

A Start with the last row of side 1 right side up and, with the second colour on your hook, slip stitch into the foundation loop from side 1.
B Chain 2 stitches.
C Double crochet into the top of the stitch from row 1/side 1 to attach.
D Turn work.
E (Cluster, chain 2, cluster) into the foundation loop of side 1.
F Treble into foundation loop.
G Double crochet into the third chain from row 1/side 1 to attach.

ROW 2

A Chain 2 stitches.
B Double crochet into the top of the stitch from row 2/side 1 to attach.
C Turn work.
D Work your first cluster of 3 trebles between the first 2 stitches.
E (Cluster, chain 2, cluster) into the corner chain space.
F Work 1 cluster into the space between the last 2 stitches.
G Treble 1 into the double crochet join of row 1.
H Double crochet into the third chain from row 2/side 1 to attach.

ROW 3

A Chain 2 stitches.
B Double crochet into the top of the stitch from row 3/side 1 to attach.
C Turn work.
D Work your first cluster between the first 2 stitches.
E Working into the space between clusters, work 1 cluster.
F (Cluster, chain 2, cluster) into the corner chain space.
G Working into the space between clusters, work 1 cluster.
H Work 1 cluster into the space between the last 2 stitches.
I Treble 1 into the double crochet join of row 2
J Double crochet into the third chain from row 3/side 1 to attach.

ROW 4

A Chain 2 stitches.
B Double crochet into the top of the stitch from row 4/side 1 to attach.
C Turn work.
D Work your first cluster between the first 2 stitches.
E Work clusters into the next 2 spaces between clusters.
F (Cluster, chain 2, cluster) into the corner chain space.
G Work clusters into the next 2 spaces between clusters.
H Work 1 cluster into the space between the last 2 stitches.
I Treble 1 into the double crochet join of row 3.
J Double crochet into the top of the stitch from row 4/side 1 to attach.
K Fasten off.

Pentagon

Let's start going beyond the square and adding more sides! The granny stitch pentagon has five sides and it will not tessellate by itself but its edges end in four clusters so it can be matched up with all the other shapes. To make this shape, you'll follow all the same techniques as for the granny square but you will start off with more clusters.

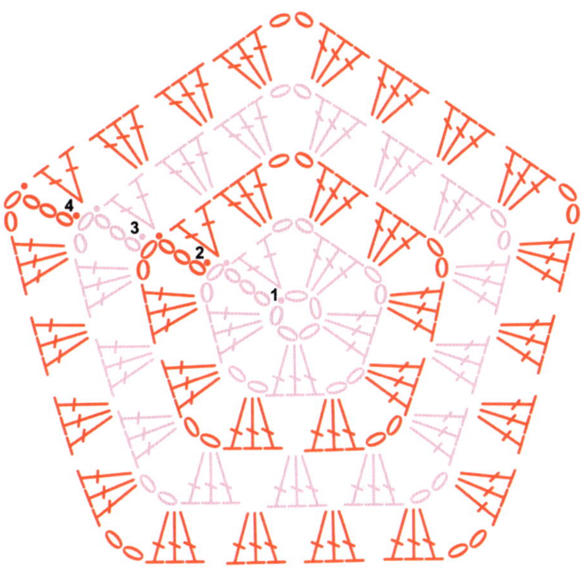

TOP TIPS

SIZING

If you are increasing the size of your shape, follow the instructions for round 4, but this time you will need to work one more cluster in the spaces along the edge for every extra round you add.

BLOCK COLOUR

If you want to work your shape in one block colour rather than a different colour each round, follow the shape's pattern omitting the fasten off from your current round and steps A and B from the next round. Replace with:

A Slip stitch into space to line up for the next round.
B Continue on with the pattern from step C.

Scan to view 'how to' video.

PENTAGON PATTERN

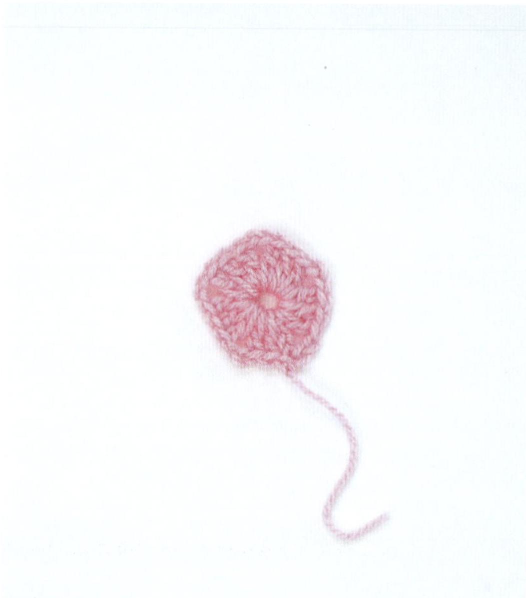

FOUNDATION

A Using your first colour, chain 5 stitches.
B Slip stitch into the first chain to form the foundation ring.

ROUND 1

A To begin the first round, chain 5 stitches. The first 3 chains of this count as a fake treble and the next 2 are the first corner. You need chains at the start to get the right stitch height at the centre of your work.
B Work 3 trebles into the centre of the ring.
C (Chain 2, treble 3) into the ring 3 times to complete the first round.
D Chain 2, treble 2, join with a slip stitch into the third chain at the start of the round to complete the round. The first chain, which creates the fake treble, and the final 2 trebles form the final cluster. From this point on, 3 trebles will be known as 1 cluster.
E To fasten off the round, create an extra chain, cut your yarn leaving a tail at least 8–10 cm (3⅛–4in) long and pull it through the loop to secure. You can leave the tail to sew in at end or use the weave-as-you-go method (see page 74).

ROUND 2

A Start with the next colour on your hook.
B Join in with a slip stitch at any chain space. Joining in new colours at different corners for each new round helps distribute where the loose yarn ends are in your shapes. It also helps with sewing the ends in neatly when finishing a shape if you are not using the weave-as-you-go method.
C Chain 5 stitches.
D Work your first cluster into the same space where you joined in.
E (Cluster, chain 2, cluster) in the following 4 corner chain spaces.
F Treble 2 into the first chain space.
G Join into the third chain at the start of the round with a slip stitch to complete the round.
H Fasten off.

ROUND 3

A Start with the next colour on your hook.
B Join in with a slip stitch at any chain space.
C Chain 5 stitches.
D Work your first cluster into the same space where you joined in.
E Working into the space between clusters, work 1 cluster.
F (Cluster, chain 2, cluster) into the corner chain space.
G Repeat steps E and F 3 more times.
H Work 1 cluster into the space.
I Treble 2 into the first chain space.
J Join into the third chain at the start of the round with a slip stitch to complete the round.
K Fasten off.

ROUND 4

A Start with the next colour on your hook.
B Join in with a slip stitch at any corner chain space.
C Chain 5 stitches.
D Work your first cluster into the same space where you joined in.
E Work clusters into the next 2 spaces between clusters.
F (Cluster, chain 2, cluster) into the corner chain space.
G Repeat steps E and F 3 more times.
H Work clusters into the next 2 spaces between clusters.
I Treble 2 into the first chain space.
J Join into the third chain at the start of the round with a slip stitch to complete the round.
K Fasten off.

Hexagon

The granny stitch hexagon has six sides. This shape will tessellate by itself and works well in combination with the squares and the octagon. This shape is worked over four rounds; however, on round 3, the positions of the corners are rotated around the shape, this tweak helps prevent the shape from distorting.

TOP TIPS

BLOCKING

When shapes have more sides, it's more likely they will distort slightly and not lie perfectly flat when taken straight off the hook. But don't worry if your hexagon looks a little wonky, that's what blocking is for! See page 93 for a guide to blocking your pieces.

SIZING

If you are increasing the size of your shape, just follow the instructions for round 4, but this time you will need to work one more cluster in the spaces along the edge for every extra round you add.

Scan to view 'how to' video.

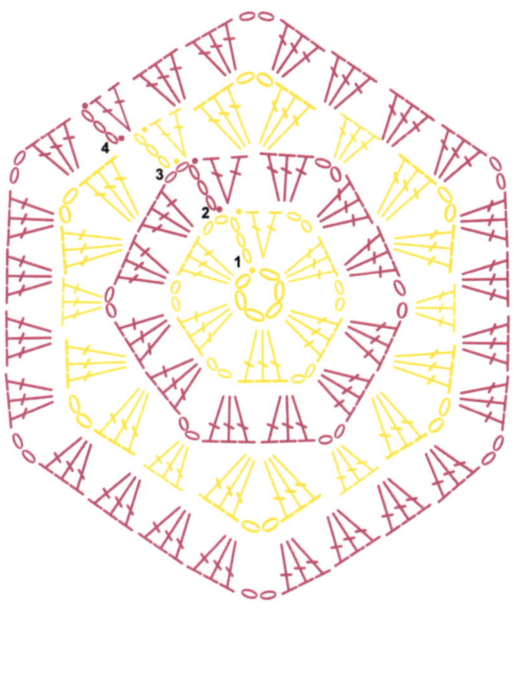

HEXAGON PATTERN

FOUNDATION

A Using your first colour, chain 6 stitches.
B Slip stitch into the first chain to form the foundation ring.

ROUND 1

A To begin the first round, chain 5 stitches. The first 3 chains of this count as a fake treble and the next 2 are the first corner. You need chains at the start to get the right stitch height at the centre of your work.
B Work 3 trebles into the centre of the ring.
C (Chain 2, treble 3) into the ring 4 times to complete your first round
D Chain 2, treble 2, join with a slip stitch into the third chain at the start of the round to complete the round. The first chain, which creates the fake treble and the final 2 trebles form the final cluster. From this point on, 3 trebles will be known as 1 cluster.
E To fasten off your round, create an extra chain, cut your yarn leaving a tail at least 8–10cm (3⅛–4in) long and pull through the loop to secure. You can either leave the tail to sew in at the end or use the weave-as-you-go method (see page 74).

ROUND 2

A Start with the next colour on your hook.
B Join in with a slip stitch at any chain space. Joining in new colours at different corners for each new round helps distribute where the loose yarn ends are in your shapes. It also helps with sewing the ends in neatly when finishing if you are not using the weave-as-you-go method.
C Chain 5 stitches.
D Work the first cluster into the same space you joined in.
E (Cluster, chain 2, cluster) in the following 5 corner chain spaces.
F Treble 2 into the first chain space.
G Join into the third chain at the start of the round with a slip stitch to complete the round.
H Fasten off.

ROUND 3

A Start with the next colour on your hook.
B Join in with a slip stitch at any chain space.
C Chain 3 stitches.
D (Cluster, chain 2, cluster) into the space between clusters.
E Work 1 cluster into the corner chain space.
F Repeat steps D and E 4 more times
G (Cluster, chain 2, cluster) into the space between clusters.
H Work 2 trebles into same space where you joined in.
I Join into the third chain at the start of the round with a slip stitch to complete the round.
J Fasten off.

ROUND 4

A Start with the next colour on your hook.
B Join in with a slip stitch in any space between clusters to the right of the corner chain space.
C Chain 3 stitches.
D (Cluster, chain 2, cluster) into the corner chain space.
E Work clusters into the next 2 spaces between clusters.
F Repeat steps D and E 4 more times.
G Work a cluster into the next space between clusters.
H Work 2 trebles into same space where you joined in
I Join into the third chain at the start of the round with a slip stitch to complete the round.
J Fasten off.

Half Hexi

The granny stitch half hexi has four sides and can be used in hexagon-based patterns to create a straight edge. Unlike the full hexagon, this shape is worked back and forth in rows. It can be worked in one block colour or multiple colours. Like the full hexagon, this shape's corner points only appear in row 3, so don't worry if you think it's making slightly the wrong shape at the start, it will reveal itself in the final row!

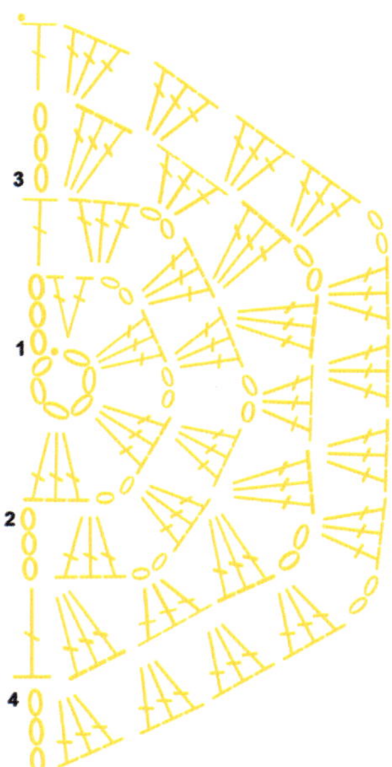

TOP TIPS

COLOUR CHANGE

As for the half 'n' half square, which is also worked in rows, you can choose to change colours for each row of the half hexi. Either join in your next colour with a single chain, or by fastening off and rejoining in the same place, as explained on page 75.

SIZING

For some of the patterns sizing is adjusted by adding extra rows/rounds. If you are increasing the size of your half hexi by one or two rounds, follow instructions for round 4, but for every extra row you will have one more cluster between spaces on the sides.

Scan to view 'how to' video.

HALF HEXI PATTERN

FOUNDATION

A Using your first colour, chain 6 stitches.
B Slip stitch into the first chain to form a foundation ring. For the rest of the shape, we will work in rows, not rounds.

ROW 1

A To begin the first row, chain 3 stitches. The 3 chains count as a fake treble stitch.
B Work 2 trebles into the centre of the ring. These stitches, along with the 3-chain fake treble, count as the first 'cluster'.
C (Chain 2, treble 3) into the ring 3 times to complete the first row. From this point on, 3 trebles will be known as 1 cluster.
D Turn.

ROW 2

A Chain 3 stitches.
B (Cluster, chain 2, cluster) in the following 3 corner chain spaces
C Treble into the top of the last treble from the row below to finish the row.
D Turn.

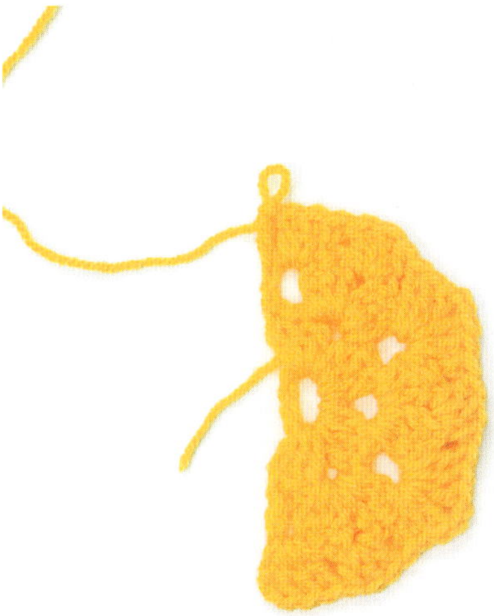

ROW 3

A Chain 3.
B Work your first cluster of 3 trebles in the space between the first 2 stitches.
C Work a cluster in the corner chain space.
D (Cluster, chain 2, cluster) into the next space between clusters to work new corner
E Repeat steps C and D once more.
F Work a cluster in the corner chain space.
G Work 1 cluster into the space between the last treble and chain stitches.
H Treble into the third chain from the row below to complete the row.
I Turn.

ROW 4

A Chain 3.
B Work your first cluster of 3 trebles in the space between the first 2 stitches.
C Work clusters into the next two spaces between clusters.
D (Cluster, chain 2, cluster) into the corner chain space.
E Repeat steps C and D once more.
F Work clusters into the next two spaces between clusters.
G Work 1 cluster into the space between the last treble and chain stitches.
H Treble into the third chain from the row below to complete the row.
I Fasten off.

Octagon

The biggest shape of the set, the octagon. This shape has eight sides and is worked over five rounds. Even though there are more rounds for this shape, its edges have four clusters so that it will match up with all the other shapes. The octagon also includes double treble crochets to achieve the correct shaping. This shape will not tessellate by itself but works beautifully with the squares and hexagons!

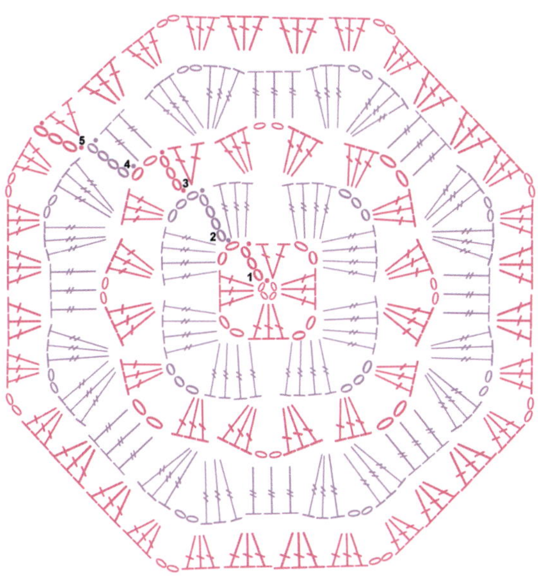

TOP TIPS

WONKY SHAPE

This larger shape can tend to distort more than the others and come out quite wonky. Remember, blocking (see page 93) is our friend and can help your shapes lay flat and even. So give it a stream or a spray to even out the sides!

LACY WEIGHT

The clusters in round 2 of this shape are made from 4 sets of double trebles, however if you wish to make your piece more light weight or give a lacy appearence you could switch these for clusters of 3 double trebles instead.

Scan to view 'how to' video.

OCTAGON PATTERN

FOUNDATION

A Using your first colour, chain 4 stitches.
B Slip stitch into the first chain to form your foundation ring.

ROUND 1

A To begin your first round, chain 5 stitches. The first 3 chains of this work as a fake treble and the next 2 are the first corner. You need chains at the start to get the right stitch height at the centre of your work.
B Work 3 trebles into the centre of the ring.
C To complete your first round (chain 2, treble 3) into the ring twice. From this point on, 3 trebles will be known as one cluster.
D Chain 2, treble 2, join with a slip stitch into the third chain at the start of the round to complete the round. To fasten off your round, create an extra chain, cut your yarn leaving a tail of at least 8–10 cm (3⅛–4in) and pull through the loop to secure.

ROUND 2

A Start with the next colour on your hook.
B Join in with a slip stitch at any chain space. Joining in new colours at different corners for each new round helps distribute the loose yarn ends around your shapes, this helps with sewing the ends in neatly when finishing a shape.
C Chain 7 stitches.
D Work 4 double treble crochets into the same space where you joined in.
E (4 double trebles, chain 3, 4 double trebles) in the following three corner chain spaces.
F Work 3 double trebles into the first chain space.
G Join with a slip stitch into the fourth chain at the start of the round to complete the round.
H Fasten off.

ROUND 3

A Start with the next colour on your hook.
B Join in with a slip stitch at any chain space.
C Chain 5 stitches.
D Work your first cluster into the same space where you joined in.
E Working into the space between clusters, work (cluster, chain 2, cluster) to create a new corner.
F (Cluster, chain 2, cluster) into the corner chain space.
G Repeat steps E and F twice more.
H (Cluster, chain 2, cluster) into the space to create a new corner.
I Work 2 trebles into the first chain space.
J Join with a slip stitch into the third chain at the start of the round to complete the round.
K Fasten off.

ROUND 4

A Start with the next colour on your hook.
B Join in with a slip stitch at any chain space.
C Chain 4 stitches
D Working into the space between clusters, work (3 double trebles, chain 2, 3 double trebles).
E Into the corner chain space, work 3 double trebles.
F Repeat steps D and E six times more.
G Working into the space between clusters, work (3 double trebles, chain 2, 3 double trebles).
H Work 2 double trebles into same space where you joined in.
I Join with a slip stitch into the fourth chain at the start of the round to complete the round.
J Fasten off.

Continues overleaf

OCTAGON PATTERN continued

ROUND 5

- A Start with the next colour on your hook.
- B Join in with a slip stitch in any space between clusters to the right of the corner chain space.
- C Chain 3 stitches.
- D (Cluster, chain 2, cluster) into the corner chain space.
- E Work clusters into the next two spaces between clusters.
- F Repeat steps D and E six times more.
- G Work cluster into the next space between clusters.
- H Work 2 trebles into same space where you joined in.
- I Join with a slip stitch into the third chain at the start of the round to complete the round.
- J Fasten off.

This shape will not tessellate by itself but works beautifully with the squares and hexagons!

Blanket (see page 98)

DESIGN AND MAKE

CRAYONS
CRAYONS
CRAYONS
CRAYONS

PLANNING YOUR PROJECT AND CUSTOMIZING DESIGNS

The aim of this book is to provide you with some fun granny shapes, great techniques and tips and tricks to follow. You may want to follow the designs exactly or you can switch them up by changing the colours or yarn choices and customizing to your heart's content!

Planning Your Project

The 15 projects in this book use a mixture of the six granny shapes presented in Chapter 2. Most projects use them in combination, working the shapes together to produce the right fit and shaping, and there are also a couple of projects that play with extending and reducing the shapes to create different sized motifs. The brilliant thing about having a design made of multiple small elements is that there's lots of room for customization: a design can be drastically changed if it's made in a different yarn type; if you join the shapes in a different way; or by altering how many colours you add to the mix. I'm all about having fun with a design and playing with colour, pattern and yarn choice – think of the designs in this book as a springboard for your own creativity, they give you an outline for a project, but you can add lots of your own personal touches to make it just right for you!

Planning Designs

Swatching and planning is an essential part of exploring the possibilities for a design – they provide a way of working out your ideas before diving into the time consuming and sometimes costly process of making. If you are going to buy that fancy yarn, you want to know exactly how much you will need and get a feel for it first! Crochet is a labour of love, embrace the slower pace of making and the fun of planning a design to work out what you want before you start.

You can dive right into the designs and colour combinations shown in each project, or remix them to create your own unique look. Get those creative juices flowing with sketching and swatching. Don't worry about being a master artist, you don't need to be Da Vinci. Using squared or dotted paper as a guide for your sketches is the perfect way to help visualize your project – it's way more efficient (and fun!) to experiment with colours and patterns on paper than through endless trial and error and ripping out rows of yarn. Personally, I love sketching and colouring a bunch of different options to find the perfect palette before I even touch my yarn stash for swatching. Depending on the design you may want to consider both colour and yarn type and it's up to you what you want to play around with first or if you explore them both in tandem.

YARN CHOICE

Sometimes, when planning a design, you will be led by colour and pattern; however, sometimes it will be yarn choice, fibre and feel. In this section I will explain some of the choices you have when considering yarn types.

On page 17, I briefly touched on the different yarns, their feel, thicknesses and basic properties, but here I will take a deeper dive into how to pick the best yarn for your projects. Switching yarn can make a big difference, and bring a whole new feeling and look to a pattern. The feel, weight and body of a finished crochet project are all hugely affected by your yarn choice.

Yarn is available in a fantastic variety of types and thicknesses but it's important to note that even within the same yarn classification, for example DK, there can be surprising variations in thickness across different brands, and especially between fibre types. These differences can affect tension and how the final project drapes and feels, so even if you have the correct yarn weight to match a project, don't just jump straight in! Trying out your yarn with a tension swatch (see page 27) to understand its properties is super important, that's why swatching is key! It's essential to match the pattern's stated tension to get the correct sizing for the piece (this is especially true for garments), and to make sure you are using roughly the same amount of yarn as stated in the pattern so that you know the quantities you will need.

Choosing Yarn

I didn't want to be too prescriptive when it came to choosing the yarn types for the designs in this book; I love leaving this choice up to the maker. This opens up some of the decision making to you, so you can consider what works best for you. Do you live in a hot or a cold climate? Are you allergic to wool? What local yarn is accessible to you? What yarn is in your price range? All of these questions can be considered when selecting your own yarn type. I also wanted to demonstrate that you can make a big difference to a piece by switching yarn. When I have got the hang of a pattern, I make it multiple times in different style yarns – I love how the end results can be so different that they feel like a different design altogether.

It's for these reasons I have only listed the yarn weight to meet the tension for each design on the patterns, and also why I've shown many of the designs in a mix of different yarns to demonstrate how yarn type can change the look and feel of a piece. However, if you do want more detailed information on the yarns I used please see page 176.

When selecting yarn for your design, think about whether you want something cool and crisp, like cotton, which is great for summer, or a fluffy texture like mohair, which holds the heat – great when it's cold. Think about how easily washable you want your piece to be, would a man-made fibre like acrylic yarn be best? Do you want the best of both worlds with a cotton–acrylic blend, which is light in weight, crisp but soft and easily washable? How large is the piece you're making? Would a more cost-effective yarn work better for this design, or are you making a smaller item where a luxury hand-spun yarn would really shine? Making these decisions will hugely affect the feel of your project and there are hundreds of yarn types out there to choose from. You can buy amazing yarns online, but if thinking about different yarn types is new to you, I recommend visiting a yarn shop so that you can give those balls a squeeze and find out firsthand what they feel like and the differences between them!

Working in one block colour to really emphasize the differences, the swatches below show the different looks and textures that can be produced by a range of yarn types.

COLOURWAYS

Colour is incredibly important to me; I love using a wide variety of colours in my work. My aim is to make you as comfortable with picking your own colour palettes as you are following the ones in this book, so in this section I'll share my top tips for exploring colourways!

What's great about the patterns in this book is that they can be customized to your liking. Whether you prefer bold, contrasting colours like me, or a more neutral palette, you have the freedom to choose the colours that best suit your style. Making your own pieces means you get to decide what colours to use!

A crochet piece doesn't need to have lots of colours, it can look just as amazing in a single colour, showing off the stitch textures or the yarn type you have selected. Or you could pick four shades of the same colour to create a tonal delight. The world's your colour oyster!

Exploring Colour

If exploring colour is new to you, you could start with the basics of colour theory by purchasing a colour wheel that highlights tonal gradients, complementary colours, split complementary colours and contrasting colours. A colour wheel with a spinning viewfinder is brilliant for breaking down which colours classically work together.

If you want to be a little more creative with your colour choices, one of my top tips is to create a mood board. Mood boards can be used to gather ideas together, so that you can start making connections to the things you are drawn to. You may want to start a sketchbook where you can play with images and colour palettes or use online platforms like Pinterest to gather images. You can also use online colour palette generators, lots of these are available for free: some work by selecting a colour palette from a photo you have uploaded and others require you to input a few colours and the generator will supply complementary colour options. These are great digital tools to explore ideas.

Create a Colour Library

I am a hands-on analogue lover when it comes to planning colour schemes. I recommend heading to your nearest DIY store to grab a bunch of paint swatch cards – these are great to play with when you're working out ideas around colourways. My tip is to punch holes in the swatch cards and you can then match your yarn scraps to the colours on the swatches by tying them on. The more yarns you have the more options you'll have to play with when planning your designs. If you do build up a big yarn reference library, it's helpful to note down the yarn types and styles on the back of the swatch for future reference.

Looking for Inspiration

When thinking about colour balance and pattern, in addition to considering which colours will feature in my designs, I like to look at the work of artists for inspiration on what proportions of colours work well together. A few of my go-tos for the projects in this book were Bridget Riley, Sonia Delaney, Matisse, Yayoi Kusama and Niki de Saint Phalle. I love the way these artists mix colour and pattern.

My final top tip for using colour is to draw inspiration from your surroundings and the things you already own. If you're crocheting a new piece of clothing, look in your wardrobe and consider your favourite pieces. Ask yourself what you love about them, what their colour palette is, and what you'd pair with a new garment. Choose colours and patterns that either match or complement your existing wardrobe to ensure that your new creation seamlessly integrates with your personal style.

Similarly, when crafting items for your home, take cues from your existing decor. Consider the colours, textures and overall style of your home. Do you prefer a minimalist look, or do you gravitate towards bold patterns and vibrant colours? Use these observations to guide your creative process and ensure that your handmade pieces feel right for you. By drawing inspiration from your surroundings and pieces you know you already love, you can create items that are both beautiful and functional for you, adding a touch of personalized charm to your wardrobe and your home.

COLOUR AND PATTERN

I have already shared my top tips on where to find inspiration for your colour palette, and now it's time to think about how to use that palette in your design and mix it in with your crochet shapes.

You can inject colour and pattern into your makes by playing around with colours and the colour balance of the rows and rounds of the shapes. The combinations you can put together are nearly endless.

In the projects in this book, I have explored working in block colour, in two colours and in broader colourways. I have also experimented with repeated patterns, bold graphic designs, classic stripes and patchwork mixes. You may wish to follow the designs, colours and patterns I have chosen or you may want to use the patterns as a loose guide and try out your own colour and pattern ideas. It's fun to explore how you can transform a design by changing just the colourway or by switching it up completely to create a piece that looks entirely different from the sample.

A great example of the iterations you can generate by only adjusting the colours used in the shapes is the monochrome jumper (see page 156). This design uses just two shades but plays around with the ordering of the black and white in the squares and hexagons within it. The summer sleeveless version uses the same four-round square for the body but is worked in a different colourway and the stripe patterning looks completely different.

As well as experimenting with the colour patterning in the individual shapes, you could also think about creating a pattern that works over multiple shapes. You can do this by combining patterns or colours to create a bigger design, like the quilt design on the cushion (see page 108) or the bold stripe in the tabard (see page 162). Exploring how the shapes work together, rather than individually, can easily be done with all the different project designs.

If you would like to follow a design but bring your own individuality to the piece by picking your own colour mix, I recommend drawing out or swatching your ideas first. A great way to play is to dig out those crayons or colouring pencils and sketch your ideas; it's a lot quicker and easier to do this on paper before you pick up a hook.

The pieces shown on the right demonstrate how you can create different colour patterns in the same makes and are intended to provide inspiration and ideas for your own projects.

CALCULATING YOUR YARN NEEDS

Planning and calculating yarn quantities for your projects can be confusing at first, but if you follow the steps below and write everything down in your design plan, it will be easy to experiment with colourways and then tally up your yarn requirements.

You'll find tension details and estimated yarn lengths listed for all of the projects in this book, making it easy to figure out how much yarn you'll need. Particular yarn brands aren't specified, just the yarn weight and tension, giving you the freedom to pick whatever yarn you like and what is accessible to you. Meterage is provided rather than yarn weight because different brands with the same weight can have varying lengths of yarn per ball. If you're curious about the yarns used in the samples, they're listed on page 176.

The approximate meterage for each project is provided for either the whole project, when worked with an even colour mix, or broken down into 'base colour' and 'contrast colour' quantities. For a few of the projects, I have also listed their colour mix in more detail to help you evenly distribute your yarn usage. Once you have chosen which project to work on and decided on your own personal colourway, you can use the number of colours you wish to use to divide the meterage totals given to work out your yarn needs.

For example, you could be making the Patchwork Jumper in a size L and need a meterage of 1835m (2006yd) for your shape colours. If you wish to use eight different colours for the shapes, then you would need to divide 1835m (2006yd) by 8. This means you would need 230m (251yd) in each colour.

Please remember that approximate meterage is just that. We all crochet with different tension, and even if our squares are the same size, the meterage can be very slightly different. If, after dividing up your quantities for your chosen yarn, you are very close to using a full ball of yarn, round it up and buy an extra ball. It's always best to err on the side of caution and have a little bit too much yarn rather than run short and lose a game of yarn chicken!

Yarn Calculation Rules

Below are some yarn calculation rules that you can use for DK/Aran weight crochet, which may come in handy if you are customizing your makes.

Granny Cluster Rows/Rounds

For every row/round of trebles you crochet, on average, you will use 14 times the length of what you are working on in yarn. Use the planned size/ length of the piece to work out the yarn quantities. For instance, if your row length is 50cm (½yd), you would need to allow for approximately 700cm/7m (7yd) of yarn.

Double Crochet Rows/Rounds

For every row/round of double crochet you work, on average, you will use 6 times the length of what you are working on in yarn. For instance, if your row length is 50cm (½yd), you would need to allow for approximately 300cm/3m (3yd) of yarn.

Double Crochet Join

If you are using the double crochet join, you will need approximately 8 times the length of what you are working on in yarn.

If you are calculating yarn for a design with a contrasting colour join, you can use the number of shapes to roughly work out the total join using this calculation:

(length of half the outer edge of shape x total number of shapes) x 8 = approximate meterage.

Open Crochet Join

If you are using the open crochet join you will need approximately 6 times the length of what you are working on in yarn.

Colour Planning: Final Round and Join

If you are planning a project with 4 round shapes and you wish to work the outer round and join in one colour for the classic look, you can use the total meterage divided by 2 to roughly work out your colour ratios between what becomes your base colour (outer round and join) and inner contrast colours.

COLOUR TECHNIQUES

Now that we have explored all the different ways the crochet shapes can be customized with different colour patterns and by switching colours on their rounds or rows, here are my tips and tricks for changing, and working with, colours in your crochet.

If, like me, you love colour, the thought of crocheting with lots of colours and all the yarn ends that will generate may be daunting. But have no fear, below I will explain my favourite ways to get your colour fix without having to spend the same length of time weaving in yarn ends as you did the making the project.

My two favourite methods are the 'travel-up' technique and the 'weave-as-you-go' method. Both these techniques were a game-changer for me when using lots of colours and reducing my finishing time.

TRAVEL-UP TECHNIQUE

This technique is brilliant if you are working with two colours and alternating between rounds, or if you are alternating between a base colour and a range of other colours.

The travel-up method involves not fastening off on each round and instead keeping the yarn live between rounds; the yarn travels up the back of the work. You can't tell this method has been used from the front of your work but it will be slightly visible from the back of your crochet, so this technique works best for pieces where you won't see both sides.

Round 1:

A Follow the shape instructions up until the final slip stitch join.

B Slip stitch join the round in the new colour (colour 2), leaving the first colour (colour 1) at the back of the work.

Round 2:

A Slip stitch into space to line up for the new round.

B Make sure not to crochet over the colour 1 yarn. Follow instructions up to the final 2 trebles of the round.

C Make sure that the colour 1 yarn on the back is caught by the final 2 trebles to minimize how much yarn you can see travelling up the back of the work. Hold the colour 1 yarn to the left (right if left-handed) and work the final trebles of colour 2 over the colour 1 yarn.

D Lift up colour 1 loosely to meet the round, slip stitch join the round in colour 1 to complete round. Do not pull the yarn too tight to make sure you keep your rounds level.

Repeat the instructions for Round 2 for further rounds to continue carrying colours up the work. If both yarns are travelling up, keep both live and do not fasten off until the end. If only one yarn is travelling up, follow the instructions but cut the yarn you're not continuing with at the end of the round. You will then only be carrying the yarn up on every other round. You can then either use the weave-as-you-go technique to tuck in the cut yarn, or leave it to the end to sew in.

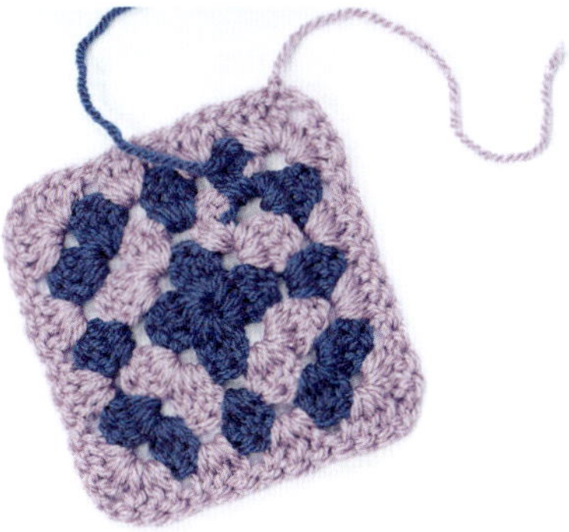

WEAVE-AS-YOU GO TECHNIQUE

This technique adds a little time to your making process but makes up for it because you won't need to weave in all your ends afterwards. This method is especially good if you're using chunky yarns where sewing in after is very difficult; however, I love this technique for all yarn types!

Join In

A Join in the new colour with a slip stitch leaving a 10cm (4in) tail.

B Using both strands – tail and attached yarn too – work the chain holding both together and following the number of chains given in your instructions. Carry both yarns for as long as the tail will go. This weaves in your yarn tail and creates a thicker chain that will match your trebles.

C If you have any tail left after your chains, you can make sure this is sticking out to the back of work and trim.

D Your tail is now woven in, continue the pattern until fasten off.

Ends Weave

A Fasten off, leaving a slightly shorter 6–8cm (2⅜–3⅛in) tail end.

B Working through the middle of the edge stitch, place your hook through the stitch from the front, hook the yarn from the back and pull it through to the front.

C Repeat this in each stitch along the edge, pulling the tail from the back through to the front, weaving it along the edge stitch. As you are working through just half the stitch this should wrap around the edge very discreetly.

D When you get to the last space between clusters your tail will reach, work through the next stitch from the back and pull the tail to the back of work.

E Trim leaving a few millimetres. Because you have ended in a gap where your next round/row will be worked this will cover any small ends sticking out.

F You have now woven in your tail and are ready to follow the pattern, repeating join-in and ends-weave techniques.

BLOCK COLOUR AND REPEATING COLOUR

Alternatively, if you want bigger blocks of one colour, all of the shapes can be made in a single colour or worked in one colour for more than one row or round.

All the shapes worked in rounds – square, pentagon, hexagon and octagon – can be continued in one colour rather than changing in the next round. Follow the shape's pattern but omit fastening off the yarn from your current round and replace steps A and B from the next round with the steps below:

A Slip stitch into space to line up for the next round.
B Continue with the pattern from step C.

CHANGING COLOURS IN ROWS

For the opposite technique, if you wish to change colours for the rows in the block colour half 'n' half square or half hexi, you can follow this easy join-in-as-you-go technique:

1. At the start of the row where you wish to switch colour, work one chain stitch in your new colour.
2. Snip the end of the previous yarn leaving a tail of 8–10cm (3⅛–4in).
3. Pull the stitch worked in the new colour tight – we do not count this in our stitch count.
4. Take both tails from new and old yarn and fold them over the working yarn before your next stitch. When you work your next chain this will pinch these ends in place and stop them from pulling loose.
5. You can then continue with the pattern instructions.

You can also choose to fasten off at the end of the row and rejoin with a slip stitch with the new colour in the same place.

1
2
3
4

JOINING TECHNIQUES

There are many ways to join the shapes in your crochet projects and everyone has their favourite, some prefer to sew, while others like the speed of a crochet join. Although most joins are interchangeable, different joins work better with different projects; your type of join can affect the look and feel of the project.

Below, you'll find details of my four favourite joins – the ones that are used in the projects in this book. To keep both camps happy, I have included two sewn styles and two crocheted methods. For sewn styles, there is whip stitch and mattress stitch and for crochet joins, double crochet closed join and double crochet open join.

For some projects, to help reduce the number of ends to weave in and make joining easier, I like to leave a long tail on my shapes and use it to join the edges of my piece. Each joining method uses varying amounts of yarn, so follow the rules given in each technique to calculate the length of your long-tail fasten off if you want to use it for joining.

1 WHIP STITCH
2 MATTRESS STITCH
3 OPEN CROCHET JOIN
4 DOUBLE CROCHET JOIN

WHIP STITCH

Creates a slanted stitch, which is flat and appears the same on both the wrong and right sides of the piece. When worked in the same colour as one of the shapes being joined, this method blends in making it a subtle join. This joining method uses a small amount of yarn and is the simplest to do.

Long-tail Fasten off: Fasten off at the last row and measure the tail length needed by going back and forth two and a half times along the edge you want to join on your shape.

STEP BY STEP

1 With right sides facing up, line up the two edges you wish to join. If you are using a long-tail fasten off, position it at the top right corner (left-hand corner if left-handed).
2 Using a tapestry needle, sew through the corner stitch.
3 Stitch through every pair of facing stitches along the edge on the right side of the work. Do not pull too tight as it might affect the tension of the shape.
4 Sew through the last corner stitch and end the stitching on the wrong side of work.
5 Fasten off by stitching through the back of the stitches in the same colour and weaving back again. To fully secure, sew in at least 8cm (3⅛in) of yarn.

MATTRESS STITCH

Mattress stitch creates an invisible join that can't be seen on either side of the work. This makes it perfect for when you are joining lots of pieces with different coloured edges together.

Long-tail Fasten off: Fasten off at the last row and measure the tail length needed by going back and forth three times along the edge you want to join on your shape

STEP BY STEP

1 With right sides facing up, line up the two edges you wish to join. If you are using a long-tail fasten off, position it at the top right corner (left-hand corner if left-handed).
2 Using a tapestry needle, sew through the corner stitch to the first join. If you don't want the stitch to be seen, sew through the centre of the corner chains rather than through the gaps.
3 Stitch through the centre of the stitch on one side first – work through the middle of the top of the stitch, through the V. Do not pull tight.
4 Sew through the facing stitch on the opposite side. Do not pull tight and leave the strand across the gap visible.
5 Travel back to the starting side, miss a stitch and sew through the middle of the next stitch. Do not pull tight and leave the strand across the gap visible.
6 Repeat Steps 4 and 5 for a few more stitches (2–3cm [½–1in] along), pinch join to hold tight and pull yarn to close the gap and connect sides.
7 Repeat step 6 until you have completed your join.
8 Fasten off end by stitching through the back of the stitches in the same colour and weaving back again. To fully secure, sew in at least 8cm (3in).

OPEN CROCHET JOIN

This crochet joining technique is worked on the wrong side of the work and creates a chain along the back with a bar-like join in the spaces between clusters, which attaches the work together. It creates an open join that mimics the openness of the granny stitch and works well to create fabric with greater drape that is perfect for clothing.

Long-tail Fasten off: Fasten off at the last row and measure the tail length needed by going back and forth eight times along the edge you want to join on your shape.

STEP BY STEP

1 Hold the two edges you wish to join together with right sides together. If you are using a long-tail fasten off, position it at the top right corner (left-hand corner if left-handed).
2 Insert the hook through the top right corner chain space of both shapes (if left-handed work left to right). If you are using a long tail, hook the yarn through the hole and secure with a double crochet. If you are using new yarn, start with the yarn on your hook and join with a double crochet.
3 Chain 3 stitches, double crochet through cluster gap of both shapes.
4 Repeat Step 3 to the corner chain space.
5 Fasten off or, if continuing to join, chain 1, double crochet into the next set of shapes' corner chain space. Repeat Steps 3–5.

DOUBLE CROCHET JOIN

This technique is a crochet joining method, it creates a firm join that has a neat finish. It is worked on the wrong side of the work and creates a slight ridge along the back of the work and a bar-like finish on the right side of the work. This method works well as a design detail and for joining large pieces as it has the same give and stretch as the crochet. This method uses more yarn than sewn joins but is often a quicker and easier way to join large pieces. You can also trap any loose outer-round yarn ends with this method and reduce the amount of ends to weave in when finished.

Long-tail Fasten off: Fasten off at the last row and measure the tail length needed by going back and forth 10 times along the edge you want to join on your shape.

STEP BY STEP

1. Hold the two edges you wish to join together with right sides facing up. If you are using a long-tail fasten off, position it at the top right corner (left-hand corner if left-handed).
2. Insert the hook through the top right corner chain space of both shapes (if left-handed work left to right). Hook the long yarn tail through the hole and secure it with a double crochet. If you are using new yarn, start with the yarn on your hook and join with a double crochet.
3. Double crochet through both layers of fabric, working into each pair of stitches along the edge.
4. Double crochet through the corner chain spaces.
5. Fasten off or, if continuing to join, chain 1, double crochet into the next set of shapes' corner chain space. Repeat Steps 3–5.

FIT, FEEL AND SIZING

One of the biggest perks of making handmade garments is getting the fit perfect – you have the control and can adjust everything! When making garments, understanding their fit and feel is important, this is where knowing your measurements comes in handy.

Measurement Guide

All the designs in this book are customizable in size, and all the clothing projects are offered in a range of sizes from XS to 5XL.

All sizes given in cm and (in).

SIZE	CHEST CIRCUMFERENCE	BODY LENGTH (CENTRE BACK TO WAIST LENGTH)	ARMHOLE DEPTH	ARM LENGTH (MEASURED CENTRE BACK TO WRIST)
XS	71–76 (28–30)	42cm (16½)	16.5 (6½)	68 (26¾)
S	81–86 (31¾–33¾)	43 (17)	17.5 (6¾)	70 (27½)
M	91–97 (35¾–38¼)	43.5 (17⅛)	19 (7½)	72 (28¼)
L	101–107 (39¾–42¼)	44.5 (17½)	20.5 (8)	74 (29⅛)
XL	112–117 (44–46)	45 (17¾)	21.5 (8½)	75 (29½)
2XL	122–127 (48–50)	45.5 (18)	23 (9)	77 (30¼)
3XL	132–137 (52–54)	45.5 (18)	24 (9½)	78 (30¾)
4XL	142–147 (56–57¾)	47 (18½)	25.5 (10)	80 (31½)
5XL	152–158 (59¾–62¼)	47 (18½)	26.5 (10½)	81 (31¾)

As well as your chest measurement, it's good to note down your body length and your centre back to wrist length to get a guide of your sleeve lengths. The table contains the average measurements for the sizes, but as we are all shaped differently, these will be affected by your height and body proportions. Picking how long you like a garment and where you like your sleeves to fall is a personal choice and can be customized when planning and making your designs.

Ease

The measurements in the size to the left show actual body measurements; ease is the allowance added to this which determines the fit of the piece. We are all different, not just in size but in how we like clothes to fit – do you like a fitted piece or that oversized feel? Use your favourite clothes to get a feel for what fit works best for you.

Each sized design in this book will state the finished piece's size, either listed as 'flat chest', 'width' or 'circumference'. These designs already have their ease added but depending on how you like your fit you may wish to size up or down depending on the design.

Tight fitting	Body skimming, your actual measurements.
Classic fit	Comfortable fit, slightly larger than actual chest measurement. Approximately 5–10cm (2–4in) more than your actual measurements.
Loose fit	Slightly oversized fit. Approximately 10–15cm (4–6in) more than your actual measurements.
Baggy/oversized	Very loose fit. Approximately 15cm+ (6in+) more than your actual measurements.

ROWS, ROUNDS AND RIBS

Adding rows, rounds and ribs are all fantastic ways to customize your projects. They can add length, create borders and give your pieces a unique look. We'll explore how to work double crochet, treble crochet, and granny cluster stitches in both rows and rounds. We'll also dive into how to work back loop double crochet rib.

Get ready to add some extra flair to your creations with these finishing touches!

DOUBLE CROCHET ROWS AND ROUNDS

Double crochet creates a tight fabric when worked in multiple rows or rounds. This simple but effective stitch is great for edging or adding length.

DOUBLE CROCHET ROUNDS

1 Work 1 double crochet stitch into each stitch (or gap between stitches, depending on the pattern).
2 To increase in the corner chain spaces work (1 double crochet, chain 1, 1 double crochet).
3 A) If you're working over the straight join of two shapes: double crochet into corner chain space, double crochet into join stitch, double crochet into corner chain space. B) If you're working over the dipped join of two shapes: double crochet 2 together over the join. To work a double crochet 2 together, put your hook into the first corner chain space, yarn over, pull through to front, leave this section on hook, put your hook in next corner chain space, yarn over, pull through to front, you will now have 3 loops on hook, yarn over and pull through all three. This closes your stitch and makes a double crochet 2 together over the join.
4 Work double crochet stitch until the end of the round and join with a slip stitch into the first double crochet to complete the round.
5 If you're repeating more rounds, chain 1 and repeat, working double crochet into each stitch and following corner increases or inner dips decreases. For working over the dip in subsequent rounds, double crochet 2 together working into the stitches either side of the double crochet together from the round below.
6 Fasten off at the desired length.

DOUBLE CROCHET ROWS

1 Work 1 double crochet stitch into each stitch (or gap between stitches, depending on the pattern).
2 To turn in the corner chain spaces work (1 double crochet, chain 1, 1 double crochet).
3 A) If you're working over the straight join of two shapes: double crochet into corner chain space, double crochet into join stitch, double crochet into corner chain space. B) If you're working over the dipped join of two shapes: double crochet 2 together over the join. To work a double crochet 2 together, put your hook into the first corner chain space, yarn over, pull through to front, leave this section on hook, put your hook in next corner chain space, yarn over, pull through to front, you will now have 3 loops on hook, yarn over and pull through all three. This closes your stitch and makes a double crochet 2 together over the join.
4 Work double crochet stitch until the end of the row.
5 If you're repeating more rows, turn your work and chain 1.
6 Repeat on the other side of the work, working double crochet into each stitch and following corner increases or inner dips decreases. For working over the dip in subsequent rounds, double crochet 2 together working into the stitches either side of the double crochet together from the round below.
7 Repeat, working back and forth following Steps 5–6 until you reach the desired length.
8 Fasten off.

GRANNY STITCH ROWS AND ROUNDS

Granny stitch rows or rounds can be used to add length to your shapes in the same style as your main stitch.

GRANNY STITCH ROUNDS

For edges or borders.

1. Join in yarn with a slip stitch in a corner chain space.
2. Chain 5, this works as a fake treble and your corner chain.
3. Work 3 trebles into the same space as the join to complete the first cluster.
4. Work 1 cluster into each gap.
5. If you are working into a corner point, work 3 treble, 2 chain, 3 treble).
6. A) If you're working over the dipped join of two shapes: work 1 treble into the first corner, work a treble 2 together over the join – place 1 part treble in each space and close, and work a final treble in second space. B) If you're working over the straight join of two shapes: work 1 cluster into each corner chain space either side of join.
7. If you're completing more rounds, repeat from Step 1. On any further rounds worked over a dipped join reduce stitches by working your cluster with treble together in each space either side of the first round's cluster and work (cluster, chain 2, cluster) in any corners.
8. Fasten off at the desired length.

GRANNY STITCH ROWS

1 Join in yarn with a slip stitch in a corner space.
2 Chain 3, this works as a fake treble.
3 Work 2 trebles into the same space as the join to complete the first cluster.
4 Work 1 cluster into each gap.
5 If you are working into a corner point, work 3 treble, 2 chain, 3 treble.
6 A) If you're working over the dipped join of two shapes: work 1 treble into the first corner, work a treble 2 together over the join – place 1 part treble in each space and close, and work a final treble in second space. B) If you're working over the straight join of two shapes: work 1 cluster into each corner chain space either side of join.
7 Work 1 cluster into each gap until the end of the row.
8 If you're repeating for more rows, chain 3, work 1 cluster into the next gap.
9 Work 1 cluster into each gap till the end of the row. On any further rows worked over the dipped join reduce stitches by working your cluster with treble together in each space either side of the first row's cluster, and work (cluster, chain 2, cluster) in any corners.
10 To complete row, work 1 treble into the 3rd chain (top of the first fake treble).
11 If repeating for more rows, repeat Steps 2–10.
12 Fasten off at the desired length.

RIB STITCH

Ribbing is usually the last stage in the making process and is mainly used for edging garments. Adding cuffs and necklines is the icing on the cake; this final step finishes off your project and gives it that final touch!

The rib stitch edging is added at the end of the make and is attached to your main piece as you go, worked in rows in the opposite direction to the edge of your work.

TOP TIP

If you want a tighter finish to a rib, just like with knitting, use the next hook size down.

DOUBLE CROCHET RIB

Ribbed stretchy edging for cuffs and necklines. The rib effect is created in crochet by working a double crochet stitch into the back loop only. This creates a fabric that has got lots of stretch and is perfect for edges. My top tip is to count while stitching to make sure you don't miss any on either end.

Foundation

A Join in yarn with a double crochet join.

B Chain the number of stitches required by the pattern plus 1 turning chain.

Row 1

A Miss 1 (turning chain), double crochet into each stitch along the foundation chain.

B Double crochet anchor into the next stitch on the project edge (anchor stitch).

C Double crochet into the next stitch along the edge (anchor stitch).

Row 2

A Turn, miss 2 (both double crochet anchor stitches).

B Back loop double crochet along the row – work stitches through the back strand of the stitch top only.

Row 3

A Turn, chain 1.

B Back loop double crochet along the row.

C Double crochet anchor into the next stitch on the project edge (anchor stitch).

D Double crochet into the next stitch along the edge (anchor stitch).

E Repeat Rows 2 and 3 until the end of the round.

Join

A On the wrong side of the work, join with a double crochet join, working through the first and last row into each stitch. Fasten off.

FINISHING

Once you've created your beautiful crochet piece, it's time to give it the finishing touches it deserves. Here, I'll guide you through the process of weaving in ends and blocking your work, ensuring a polished look. Once you've mastered these techniques, you'll be ready to show off your creations with pride!

Weaving in Yarn Ends

Dealing with your yarn ends is a bit like tidying up after making a big creative mess. It's boring but it's a necessary evil – it ensures all your hard work doesn't unravel. If you're working on a project with multiple motifs – or lots of colour – it's a good idea to weave in your ends as you go. This will make the final finishing process much easier.

You can use a tapestry needle to weave your yarn ends into the fabric. When fastening off, leave a tail of at least 10cm (4in) so that you can sew in a minimum of 8cm (3⅛in) of yarn. It's also good to remember that if you're edging in double crochet or joining with a solid double crochet join, these ends can be trapped in the stitching to avoid sewing in. Sewing in your ends with a tapestry needle is the most common method but you can also use a latch hook (which I find a brilliant and speedy way to sew in your ends if you have lots of colour changes like me). Follow these top tips for good results:

- Sew ends in on the wrong side of the crochet fabric.
- Try to stitch into the same colour yarn to secure discreetly.
- Weave through the stitches in one direction for a short distance and then turn back on yourself, weaving through in the other direction.
- Try to sew through some of the yarn, splitting the stitch/tail to create invisible knots.
- Snip away any excess.

Blocking

Blocking is a technique that involves wetting or steaming your crochet piece to shape and set it into place so that it lies flat and keeps its shape. It's like giving your project a spa treatment! Blocking helps to even out tension, straighten stitches and create a polished finish. It's especially helpful for projects that have become misshapen during the making process. While not all projects require blocking, it can significantly enhance the appearance of many pieces. Blocking is the final action in the making process and my recommendation is to block a project after it has been joined/finished.

THE BLOCKING PROCESS

You can either dampen your work by washing it, by using a water spray or by using a steam iron. I am a lazy blocker, so I tend to use a steam iron. If you do use a steam iron the most important rule is to always turn your work inside out or onto the wrong side to block. If you are using a particularly delicate yarn such as cashmere, it's best to be cautious and opt for the water spray rather than steam. On almost all occasions the steam iron should never touch your fabric! However, some stiff cottons or raffias will benefit from being pressed by an iron, for these always use a teatowl in between the iron and the piece and test the process on a small sample first before trying it on a finished piece!

1. The shapes/garments should be pinned out to the correct size on an ironing board or a foam block (foam play mats sold for use by children are ideal for this purpose) using large-headed pins. Particular attention should be paid to any seams or joins to ensure the finished item has crisp, straight edges.
2. Once pinned, the motifs/garments should be dampened either by spraying with water or holding a steam iron at least 10cm (4in) above the fabric and steaming it liberally. Make sure the fabric feels damp to the touch. If you are not pinning the work (because it's large or a garment), once it's damp, it can be pulled and flattened into the correct shape. Ensure the steam iron never touches the crocheted item as the fibres can be permanently changed or damaged by the heat. The crochet should then be left to dry flat before the pins are removed.

CROCHET CARE

After mastering your make and spending time and love on your crochet pieces, it's important to give them the care they deserve! These tips and tricks will help you to care for your crochet so your makes can last a lifetime.

Storage

Storing your crochet correctly will ensure it does not stretch and keep it safe from moths. Although you may want to display any garment you have made in pride of place in your wardrobe, do not hang them up and follow the tips below.

- Crocheted garments should always be stored folded and flat, never hung as they will droop and stretch after a while.
- If your crocheted items are made from natural fibres, clothes moths can be an issue. If you are storing any pieces for a long time I recommend airtight vacuum bags, these will help keep any nasties away from your natural fibre makes.
- If you ever suspect moths have gotten into any of your woolly or natural fibre pieces, put them in a bag in the freezer for four days to kill the larvae. Inspect the crochet for any holes and darn them where needed.

Washing Crochet

We wash items far too often, so if only a small area of your crochet is dirty, spot cleaning is recommended; however, sometimes it will be necessary to wash the entire garment. Follow these tips.

- Always refer to the ball band to find the correct washing instructions for the yarn that has been used. This will avoid any shrinking dilemmas if you're using a natural yarn!
- If in doubt, always wash carefully by hand in cool water, using a detergent suitable for delicate items.
- Do not wring out wet items, instead remove any excess water by rolling them in a clean, dry towel.
- If you are using a washing machine, use the most delicate setting or the wool setting and the lowest spin speed. For smaller items it is always a good idea to place them in a laundry bag or pillowcase in the machine.
- Always dry items flat and out of direct sunlight.

Mending

Mending your makes right away if you see a small hole or loose end will catch minor damage before it has a chance to become more extensive.

- Loose ends can be woven back into the fabric with a tapestry needle or latch hook. If the loose end is very short and too small to thread through a needle normally, start by weaving the needle itself through the crochet piece, eye-end first, to meet the loose end. Then place the yarn tail through the eye to thread the needle and pull through to re-secure your loose end.
- My final top tip is to use a de-bobbling tool, these work as a razor and take off any pilled yarn bobbles that have formed due to friction. This tool will help your creations to stay looking freshly made.

Shape It Up Blanket 98
Beret 104
Cushion Cover 108
Knot Bag 112
Collar 116
Perfect Pouch 120
Neckerchief Scarf 124
Cozy Cowboy Slipper Socks 128
Floor Cushion Cozy 134
Simple Squares Shopper 140
Colour Lovin' Coatigan 144
Bonnet 152
Patchwork Jumper 156
Tabard 162
Vest 168

THE PROJECTS

Shape It Up Blanket

This blanket makes use of four of our shapes: the octagon, the hexagon, the half hexi and a slight twist on the granny square that helps to fit them all together. The shapes tessellate to make a beautiful patchwork-style blanket that looks like an intricate tiled floor. It's the perfect size for a sofa, single bed or the foot of a double bed, and because it's worked in chunky yarn it grows quickly for a large-scale project!

TOP TIPS

This project is easily extendable: increase the number of row repeats or how many shapes there are across the width to create a larger blanket.

Why not try making a smaller baby or lap blanket in DK yarn? If you wish to make a squarer blanket, rather than rectangular, you can also miss the first and last hexi/square rows and start and end on the octagon rows.

YARN WEIGHT
Chunky (bulky)

HOOK SIZE
8mm/US size L-11
(or to match tension)

TENSION
One three-round amended square = 14 x 14cm (5½ x 5½in)
Hexagon, flat edge to flat edge = 20.5 (8⅛ x 8⅛in)
Octagon, flat edge to flat edge = 28 cm (11 in)

SIZE
One size = 155 x 128cm (61 x 50½in)

SAMPLES
Two design variations are shown, both worked in chunky acrylic yarn:

Variation 1: Cream base colour with bright colour pops in five contrast colours.

Variation 2: Colour block variation, with the final round of shapes and first round of the octagon in black base colour. The rest of the design is worked with nine randomly mixed contrast colours.

APPROXIMATE METERAGE
Total: 1885m (2062yd)
See chart for variation 1 meterage breakdown

TOTAL SHAPES
12 octagons
16 small squares
12 hexagons
Eight half hexis

12 16 12 8

SHAPE IT UP BLANKET

Step by Step Pattern Guide

THE GRANNY SQUARE HAS THREE ROUNDS ONLY, THE FOURTH ROUND HAS FOUR TREBLES TO A CLUSTER

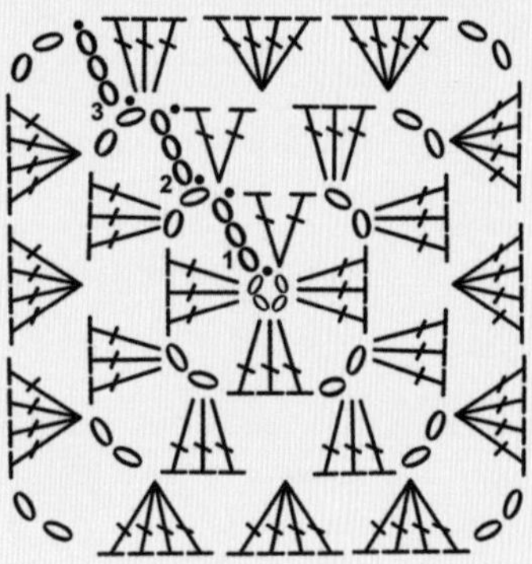

PLAN YOUR DESIGN – IF YOU ARE WORKING VARIATION 1 FOLLOW COLOUR ORDER

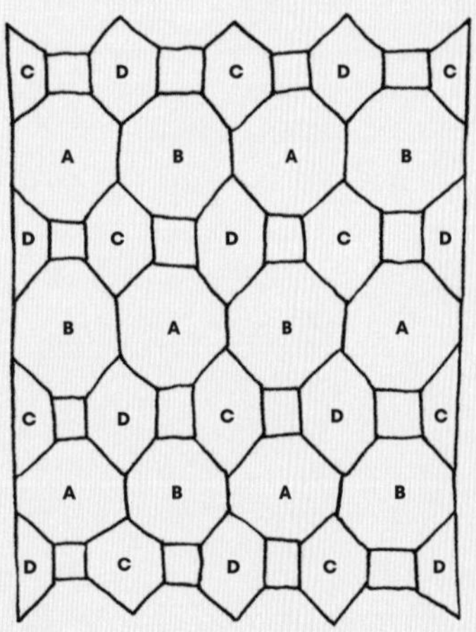

JOIN THE SQUARE AND HEXAGON ROWS

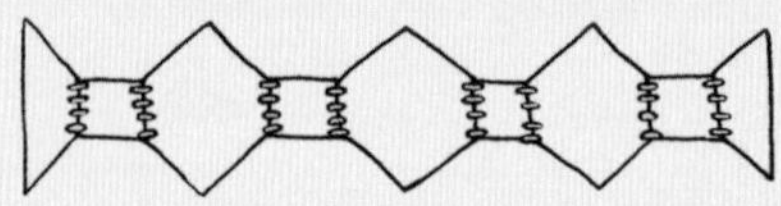

x 4

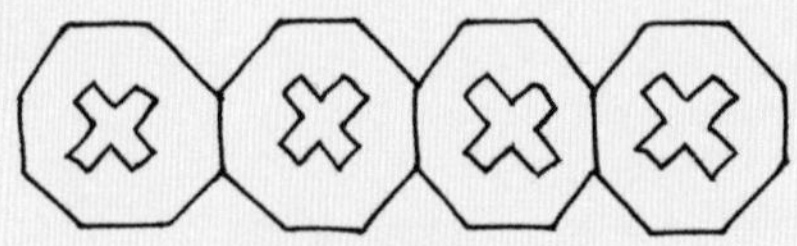

x 3

JOIN THE HEXI/SQUARE ROWS TO THE OCTAGON ROWS

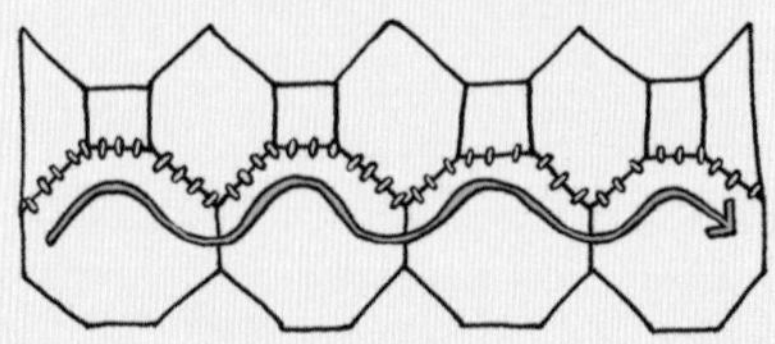

ADD THE EDGING

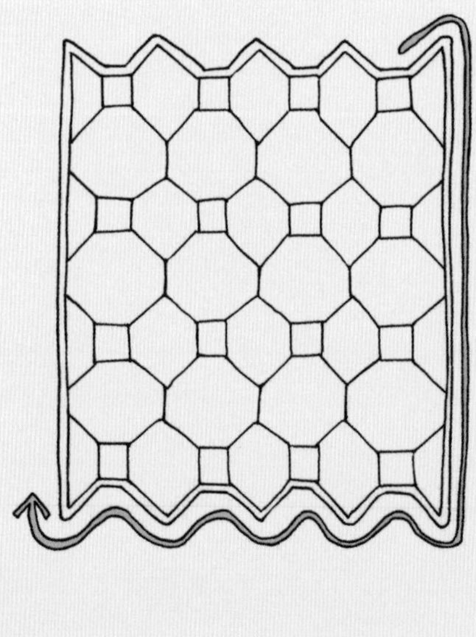

Getting Started

SHAPES

Make 12 octagons, 12 hexagons, eight half hexis and 16 small squares. The small square is worked over three rounds, but there is a slight twist in the third round. To get the shapes to fit together nicely when joined, the square needs to be a round smaller than usual but to have the same stitch count as a four-round square. To do this, follow the square pattern for rounds 1 and 2, but for round 3, change and work four trebles to a cluster. This will give each side of your square a treble stitch count of 12. This will allow your shapes to fit together brilliantly and lie flat after blocking. Because we will be using new yarn to contrast join the shapes in a double crochet join, your shapes can be fastened off with short tails.

COLOURWAY

If you are following the variation 1 colour balance, follow the colour order in the chart below for your shapes' rounds/rows and use the diagram opposite for your shapes' placement and order. For your small, three-round squares, work the first round in a contrast colour and rounds 2 and 3 in your base colour, use your contrast colours evenly for these square centres and evenly distribute them in the blanket. If you are following variation 2, use the meterage in the table as a guide. Divide the contrast colour total amount by how many colours you wish to use – refer to the calculations on page 71 to help you.

	A	B	C	D
Round 1	Colour 4	Colour 5	Colour 1	Colour 3
Round 2	Colour 3	Colour 2	Base Colour	Base Colour
Round 3	Base Colour	Base Colour	Colour 4	Colour 1
Round 4	Colour 2	Colour 3	Colour 2	Colour 5
Round 5	Colour 1	Colour 4	–	–

Instructions

JOINING

Square and Hexagon Rows

A Using your joining/base yarn colour and the double crochet joining method (see page 81), join the shapes together to create 4 rows, following the colour order in your chosen variation.

B Your row should be 9 shapes wide and follow the order: half hexi, square, hexagon, square, hexagon, square, hexagon, square, half hexi.

C Place shapes right sides together to join along the wrong side of the work.

D Start in corner chain spaces of both shapes and work along the back of the piece. Even though the squares have fewer rounds than usual, their stitch count is the same as the hexagons and half hexis, so work through each stitch when joining.

E Open out and join the next shape using the same method.

F Repeat until you have created a full row.

G Repeat this process until you have 4 rows following the colour order in the diagram.

Octagon Rows

A Using your joining/base yarn colour and the double crochet joining method, join the octagons together. Create 4 rows, following the colour order.

B Your row should be 4 shapes wide. Make sure that the octagon centres are rotated so that there is an 'X' at the centre rather than a '+'.

C Place shapes right sides together to join along the wrong side of the work.

D Start in corner chain spaces of both shapes and work through each stitch along the back of the piece.

E Open out and join the next shape using the same method.

F Repeat until you have created a full row.

G Repeat this process until you have 4 rows following the colour order in the diagram.

	VARIATION 1						VARIATION 2	
	BASE COLOUR ROUNDS, JOINS, EDGING	**COLOUR 1**	**COLOUR 2**	**COLOUR 3**	**COLOUR 4**	**COLOUR 5**	**BASE COLOUR** ROUNDS, JOINS, EDGING	**CONTRAST COLOURS**
METERAGE (YD)	725 (793)	260 (285)	215 (235)	275 (301)	280 (306)	130 (142)	935 (1023)	950 (1039)
TOTAL METERAGE (YD)	1885 (2062)							

Blanket Join

A Using your base colour on the wrong side of the work, use the double crochet joining method (see page 81) to attach your hexi/square rows to your octagon rows.
B Use stitch markers to hold the crochet in place by matching the corner points.
C Start in the half hexi corner point space and join with a double crochet into the octagon corner space.
D Double crochet through both layers up to the next hexagon corner chain space.
E In the corner, work one double crochet through the hexagon corner and the octagon corner chain space.
F Work into the next square corner chain space and then back into the same octagon corner chain space, joining with a double crochet.
G Work double crochet along the edge until you reach the next square corner chain space.
H Double crochet through the square corner chain space and into the octagon corner chain space.
I Double crochet through the next hexagon corner chain space and then back into the same octagon corner chain space.
J Double crochet through both layers up to the next hexagon corner chain space.
K In the corner, work one double crochet through the hexagon corner and the octagon corner chain space.
L Work back through the same hexagon corner chain space and into the next octagon corner chain space.
M Repeat steps D to L until you have worked all the way along the row. On your final repeat you will end on step J.
N Fasten off.

EDGING

A Using your base colour, join in at any edge corner space.
B Following the double crochet rounds instructions on page 86, work 2 edging rounds.
C When working on the sides of the half hexis, place 2 double crochets over each side of a treble stitch and in the centre ring, to evenly space across the shape.
D Fasten off after 2 rounds.

FINISHING

A Sew in any remaining yarn ends.
B Block following the instructions on page 93.

Beret

In my opinion there is no outfit that isn't enhanced by a beret! They are the perfect piece to have in multiple colours to go with every outfit. A combination of squares and a hexagon are used to create the shape of this beret and it's finished off with rib stitch. A smaller hook than is recommended for the yarn type is used to give this piece a close tension, creating a thick, cozy crochet fabric!

YARN WEIGHT
Chunky (bulky)

HOOK SIZE
5mm/US size H-8
(or to match tension)

TENSION
One single square motif = 12 x 12cm (4¾ x 4¾ in)

SIZE
One size = 29cm (11½in) hat diameter

SAMPLES
Two design variations are shown (both worked in open crochet join):

Variation 1: Block colour – worked in chunky chenile yarn
Variation 2: Two-colour stripe – using 2 strands of DK yarn worked together to create chunky yarn. Using a base colour and 5 contrast colours If using 2 strands you will need to double the meterage.

APPROXIMATE METERAGE
Total: 185m (203yd)
Base colour: 75m (82yd)
Contrast colour: 115m (126yd)

TOTAL SHAPES
Six squares and one hexagon.

6 1

BERET

Step by Step Pattern Guide

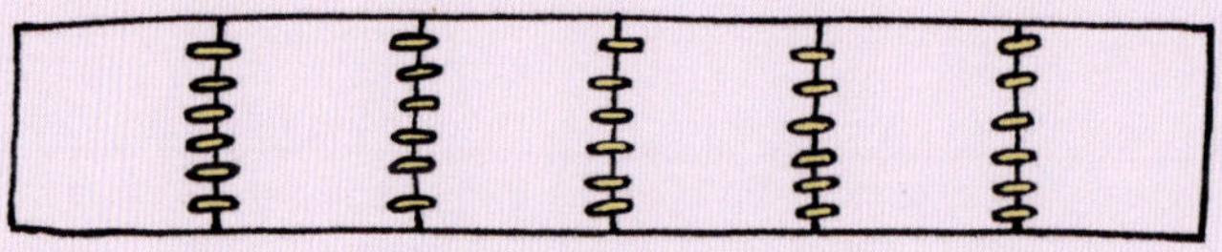

BERET BRIM JOIN

BERET BRIM

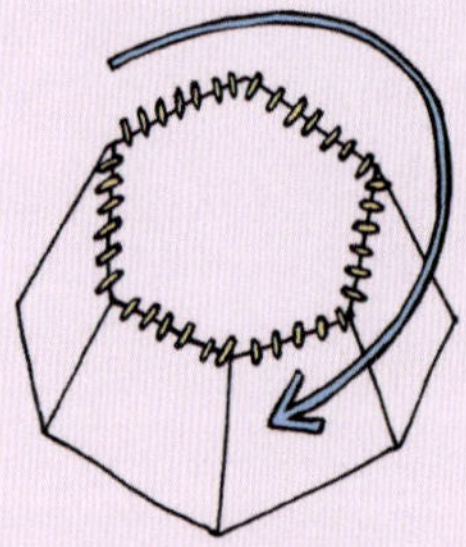

BERET TOP JOIN

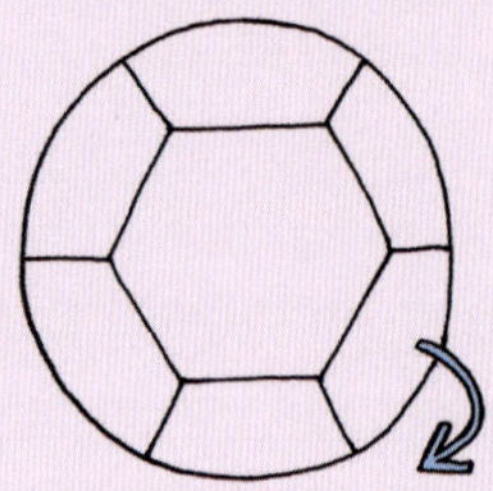

TURN RIGHT WAY ROUND AND FOLD IN BRIM EDGES TO HALFWAY POINT

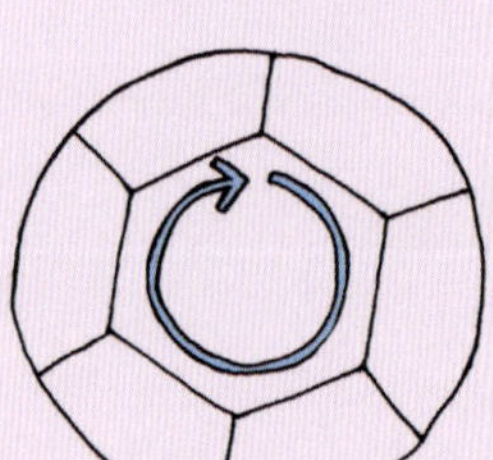

EDGE TRIM

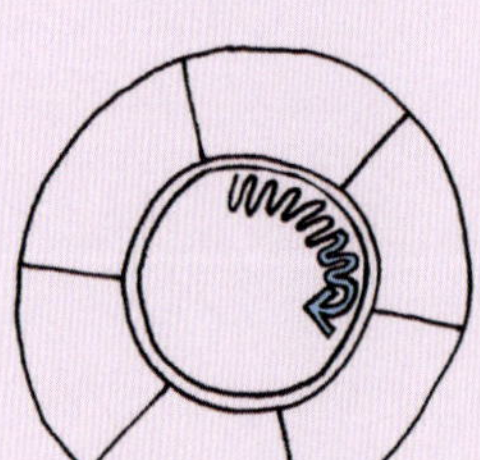

BERET RIBBING

TOP TIPS

To get the perfect beret shape, wet the beret and block it by placing a dinner plate inside it and balancing the plate on a cup inserted through the hat opening. Leave to dry.

To get the perfect head opening that won't stretch, sew a strand or two of shirring elastic through the back of the stitches on the inside of the rib. This will give the head opening some extra stretch.

Getting Started

SHAPES

Make six squares, and one hexagon. It's best to seam this project with an open crochet join (see page 80), but all join types will work. Fasten off all squares with the length of tail determined by the join you wish to use (see pages 76–81).

COLOURWAY

Colour order for shapes, if working the two-colour option:

- Round 1: contrast colour (use travel-up colour technique, see page 73)
- Round 2: base colour
- Round 3: contrast colour
- Round 4: base colour

Instructions

JOINING

Beret Brim Join

A Using your long tails and an open crochet join, join your squares into a strip of 6.
B Use the tail on the final square to join your strip to create a continuous loop.

Beret Top Join

A Working in the same colour as your shape's last round, join the beret brim to the hexagon to create the hat top. Remember to join on the wrong side (inside the hat). You can use stitch markers to hold the pieces together while you work.
B With the yarn on your hook, join in by placing a double crochet join through both layers. Start at any square corner chain space right of the join (left of join if left-handed) and any hexagon corner chain space to join both layers together.
C Work into the next square corner chain space and back into the same hexagon corner chain space with a double crochet.
D Continue joining with the open crochet join until the next square corner.
E Work one double crochet through the square corner and hexagon corner.
F Work the next double crochet through the next square corner and back into same hexagon corner.
G Repeat steps D to F until you reach your first crochet join.
H Slip stitch into the first stitch to join the round.
I Fasten off.

Beret Edge Trim

A Turn the beret right side out so the joins are on the inside.
B Work 1 round of double crochet (see page 86) around the open edge of your beret.
C Starting with the yarn on your hook, join in with a double crochet in the top of the treble stitch to the right of a corner chain space (left stitch if left-handed).
D Double crochet 2 together in the 2 corner chain spaces either side of the join. Work the first part of your first double crochet in the first corner and work another first part of a double crochet in the next corner, complete the dc2tog to reduce 2 stitches into 1 over join.
E Double crochet in the next 6 stitches.
F Miss 1 stitch.
G Double crochet in the next 5 stitches.
H Repeat steps D to G until you work your way round to your joining stitch.
I Slip stitch in the first double crochet to join.
J Keep the yarn live, do not cut.

Beret Rib

A Continue working in the live yarn.
B Work rib around the edge (following instructions on page 91).
C Start with a chain of 4 to make a rib of 3 stitches.
D When you have attached rib to the entire double crochet edge, fasten off leaving a 15-cm (6-in) tail.
E Use the long tail and a tapestry needle to join the first and last rib rows to create a continuous rib edge.
F To keep the rib from stretching out either use elastic as stated in the top tips, or work a loose slip stitch around the edge of the rib on the wrong side of the work to give your edge less stretch. Before fastening off, check size on the head, if it's the wrong size adapt the slip stitch tension to fit.

Finishing

A Sew in any remaining yarn ends
B Block the piece to finish.

TOP TIP

This envelope-style construction also makes the perfect laptop or book cover if you use smaller squares. Make a test square and measure it to work out how many you would need to create a different sized envelope.

Cushion Cover

This envelope-style cushion cover with tie detailing is amazingly versatile and adaptable. You can use either of the square patterns – the granny square or half 'n' half – or even combine them to make your own unique design. Customize your colour choices, design pattern and join methods to suit you. Grab your hook, it's time to whip up new covers for all your existing cushions!

YARN WEIGHT
Aran (worsted)

HOOK SIZE
5mm/US size H-8
(or to match tension)

TENSION
One single square motif =
11 x 11 cm (4¼ x 4¼in)

SIZE
One size =
44 x 44cm (17¼ x 17¼in)
To fit cushion pad =
48 x 48cm (19 x 19in)

SAMPLES
Two design variations are shown, both worked in DK acrylic yarn:

Variation 1: Quilt-style design with a mix of granny squares and half 'n' half squares. White is used as a base colour and is also used for open crochet joining and edging. Four contrast colours are also used.

Variation 2: Half 'n' half squares create a bold, graphic design using a bright colour mix of eight colours and black as a contrasting joining colour, worked with a double crochet join.

APPROXIMATE METERAGE
Total: 635m (695yd)
Square colours: 560m (613yd)
Contrast join and edging colour: 75m (83yd)

TOTAL SHAPES
Thirty-two squares.

32

CUSHION COVER

Step by Step Pattern Guide

PLAN YOUR DESIGN – IF YOU ARE WORKING THE QUILT DESIGN FOLLOW COLOUR ORDER.

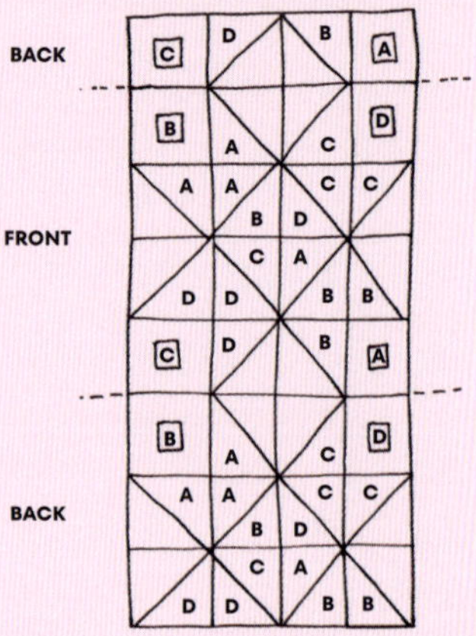

PIN CORNERS TOGETHER AND JOIN SHORT ROWS

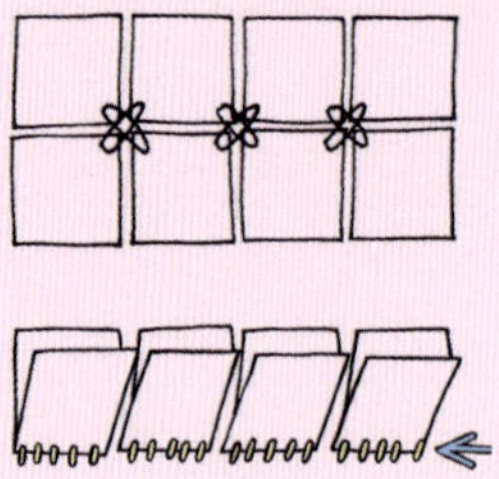

WORK ALONG ADDING MORE ROWS AND JOINING

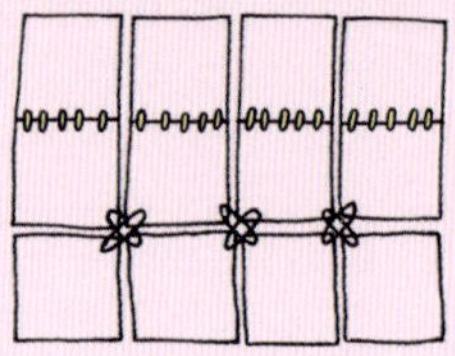

JOIN ALONG LONG STRIPS

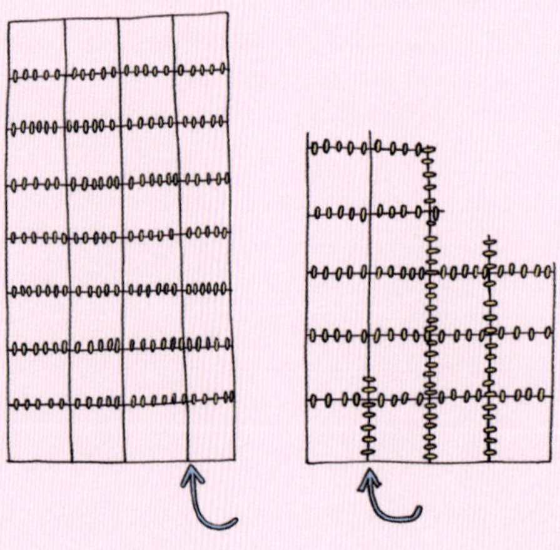

FOLD RIGHT SIDES TOGETHER.

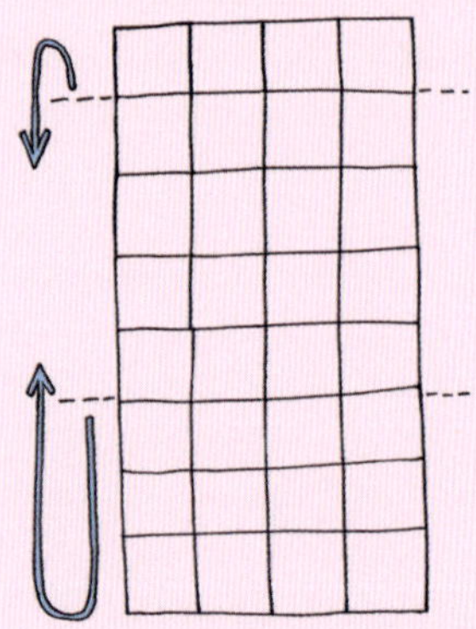

JOIN ALONG EDGES ON INSIDE, TO MAKE ENVELOPE.

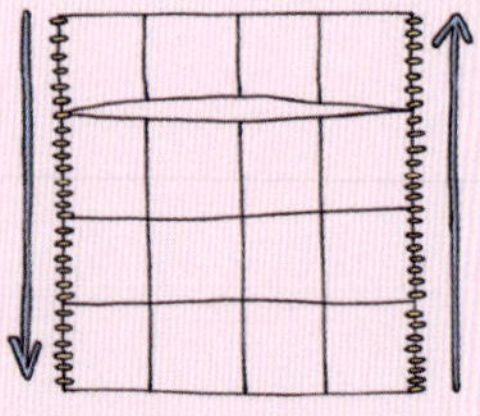

TURN RIGHT WAY OUT AND EDGE OPENING MAKING TIES.

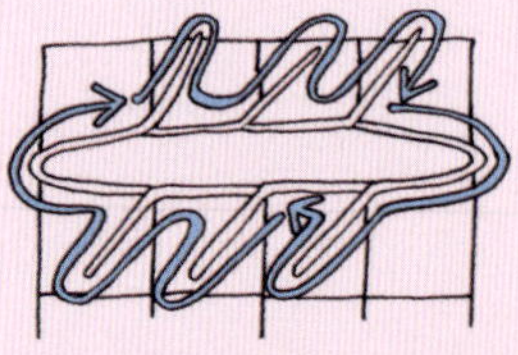

PLACE YOUR CUSHION PAD INSIDE AND TIE THE BOWS TO COMPLETE.

Getting Started

SHAPES

Make 32 squares, 16 for the front and 16 for the back. You can use either of the square patterns for this project – granny or half 'n' half. If you are following the quilt-style design, make eight granny squares and 24 half 'n' half squares. Both samples use a different yarn colour for a contrasting join but if you are working in granny squares you can also use the long tail fasten off for your chosen join style if you wish. Any join can be used for this project, but the double crochet joins (see pages 80–81) work well.

COLOURWAY

For the quilt style design, make your 24 squares following the contrast colour breakdown in the table below. You will also have eight granny squares. Work row 1 in contrast colour and rows 2–4 in the base colour, make two in each colour. Follow the diagram for the layout.

QUANTITY	SIDE 1	SIDE 2
2	A	Base Colour
2	A	B
2	C	Base Colour
2	C	D
2	B	Base Colour
2	D	Base Colour

Instructions

JOINING

Square Joining

A Lay out the squares in your panel to make sure your chosen design is in order.

B Join the squares together using any of the four joining techniques (see pages 76–81).

C First, join the short square edges into rows and then join the long rows together. If you have used the granny square, you can use long tail fasten offs for your short edge joins. For half 'n' half squares, or a mix of the two styles, use the new yarn to join. Use stitch markers to join the corners of the squares together while you join them. Pin the squares as you work, rather than pinning the whole piece at once.

D Join the shorter rows for the width of the cushion first.

E Then join the longer rows for the length of cushion's front and back.

F Fasten off and sew in yarn ends.

Side Joins

A Fold right sides together.

B Fold down the first row at the top and fold up the bottom 3 rows to create an envelope.

C Using your chosen joining method, work through both layers along the edges to join each side.

D Turn the cushion cover the right way out.

Edging and ties

A Using the joining colour yarn, start in the corner chain space of the opening square that meets the edge with a double crochet.

B Work double crochet into each stitch up to the corner chain space.

C Chain 21.

D Turn and slip stitch 20 through the back bump of 20 chains.

E Double crochet into next square's corner.

F Repeat steps B to E twice more to make 3 ties along the edge.

G Double crochet along the edge up to the corner chain space.

H Work 1 double crochet in the corner, rotate cushion and work 1 double crochet in the corner chain space of the square on the other side of the opening.

I Repeat steps B to G to complete ties along the second edge.

J Double crochet in the corner chain space.

K Slip stitch join into the first stitch to complete the round.

L Fasten off.

Finishing

A Sew in any remaining yarn ends.

B Block if desired.

C Insert the cushion pad and tie small bows with the ties to secure.

TOP TIP

You can easily adapt this cover style for larger or smaller cushions – you can add more squares or change your yarn thickness to affect the size. Remember, you want your cover to be a little smaller than your cushion pad so it looks nice and plump!

Knot Bag

This nifty knot bag is the perfect accessory to hang off your arm! This make uses a clever combination of the six shapes to produce the bag shape and is the perfect mini shopper – or if you loop one strap through the other, a Japanese-style knot bag. Make it in an Aran-weight cotton for a brilliant day bag or work in a glitzy ribbon yarn for the perfect party bag!

YARN WEIGHT
Aran (worsted)

HOOK SIZE
5mm/US size H-8
(or to match tension)

TENSION
One single square motif = 10.5 x 10.5cm (4 x 4in)

SIZE
One Size = 28cm (11in) across bag body, flat

SAMPLE
Design is worked in glitter tape yarn with black as its base colour and 4 contrast colours. Alternative sample in 2 colours seen on page 87. Worked in aran cotton on a 5.5mm/US size I-9 hook for a slightly bigger bag (30cm [11¾in])

APPROXIMATE METERAGE
Total = 285m (312yd)
Base colour = 135m (148yd)
Contrasting colour = 150m (164yd)

TOTAL SHAPES
Five squares
Two half hexis
Two octagons
Six mini, three-round squares

5 2 2 6

TOP TIPS

If you're worried about losing any of your smaller bits through the holes in this style of bag you can line the body of the bag. Many online yarn companies send out their yarn in thin organza bags and these make the perfect ready-made linings to tack into place in a make, or a tote bag works as a great liner too!

KNOT BAG

Step by Step Pattern Guide

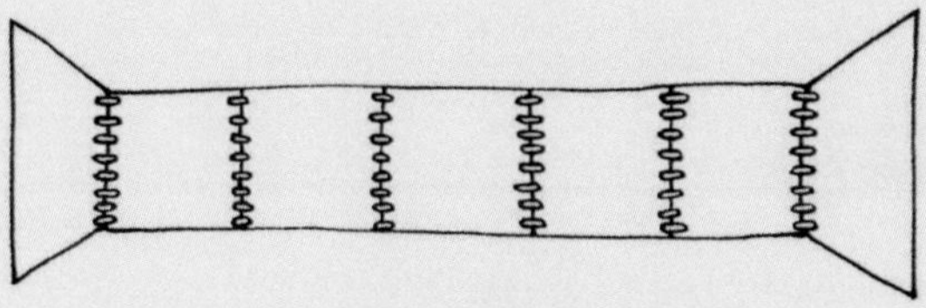

BAG GUSSET

BAG JOIN

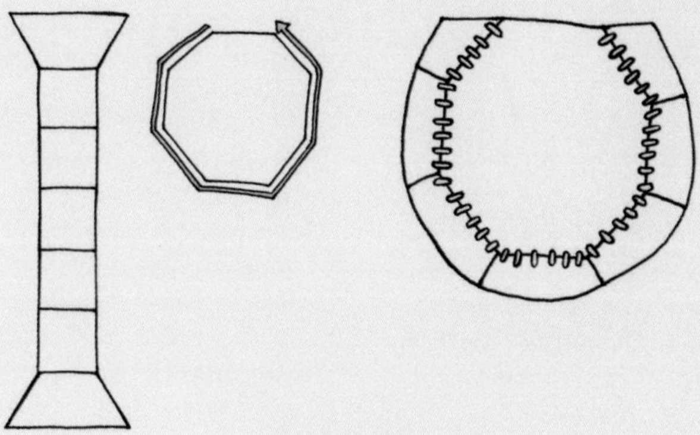

STRAP JOIN X 2

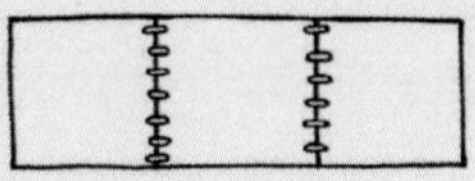

STRAP JOIN

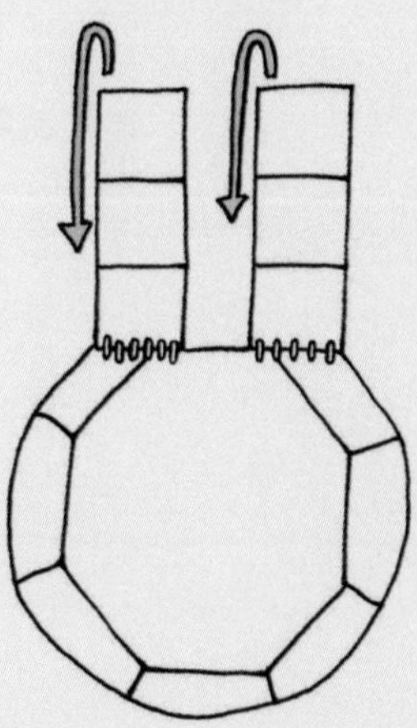

BAG EDGING

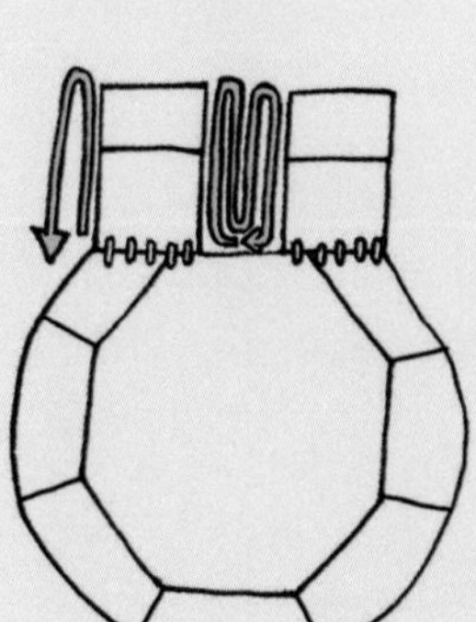

Getting Started

SHAPES

Make five squares, two half hexis, two octagons and six mini, three-round squares. When making your half hexis on your final row, complete the shape by working double crochet across the longer half edge. Chain 1 at start, then work 2 double crochets over each side of trebles and in centre ring, fasten off in 3rd chain from start of row to complete as a round. This project works best with a solid join – I recommend the double crochet join (see page 81) for a sturdier bag. Fasten off all shapes with the long tail length for this join.

COLOURWAY

- Work the bag in any colour combination you wish, but pattern works best when ending each shape in the same colour and using this for your join too.
- Sample is worked with black as a base colour and 4 contrast colours. Octagon is worked in all colours stripe ending with base colour. Squares are worked in 1 contrast colour and then ended with final round in base colour.

Instructions

JOINING

Bag Gusset

A Using your long yarn tails and a double crochet join, join your squares into a strip of five.

B Use the long tail from your final square to join the bottom edge of your half hexi to your strip of squares.

C Using your base colour, join the remaining half hexi to the other end of your square strip to complete the bag gusset. because you do not have a long tail to join with here, start with the yarn on your hook and join in by putting the corner chain spaces together, then continue across with double crochet.

Bag Body Join

A Working in your base colour and following the order on the diagram, join the bag gusset to the first octagon. Remember to join on the wrong side of the work (inside the bag). Use stitch markers to hold the pieces together while you join.

B Start with the base colour on your hook, and work through your octagon corner chain space and into the first stitch of your half hexi edge.

C Double crochet into each stitch, through both layers, until you reach the next corner chain space.

D Work 1 double crochet through the octagon corner chain space and into the half hexi corner chain space.

E Work your next double crochet through the same octagon chain space but this time on the other side, and through the first square's corner chain space.

F Double crochet up to the next corner chain space of your octagon and work a double crochet through the octagon and first square's corner.

G Work your next double crochet stitch back through the octagon and into the next square's chain space.

H Repeat this until you have worked through all the squares of the gusset and the last half hexi, leaving one side of the octagon open.

I Fasten off

Repeat this on the opposite side to join the second octagon.

Strap Join

A Join two sets of three mini squares together with double crochet to create the straps.

B Line your straps up at the edge of your bag, leave the centre stitch of your half hexi free and join the strap from the next stitch over.

C Double crochet across the strap to join to the bag.

D Fasten off.

E Fold the strap over and join in the same place on the opposite side, leaving the centre stitch of the half hexi free and joining from the next stitch over – I find it easiest to work from the outside in to make sure your stitches line up.

F Fasten off.

Repeat to join the second strap.

Bag Edging

Work one round of double crochet around the open edges of your bag.

A For the outer straps, join in the base colour yarn with a double crochet join in the free centre stitch of the half hexi, work one round and slip stitch into the first double crochet to complete the round, fasten off. Repeat on the other outer strap.

B For the inner strap, join in the base colour yarn with a double crochet join in at the start point of one of your straps, work one round and slip stitch into the first double crochet to complete round, fasten off.

Finishing

A Sew in any remaining yarn ends.

B Block piece to finish.

Collar

A collar can be the perfect finishing touch to any outfit; drape it over your favourite top, add instant chic to a simple tee, or bring that cute prairie style to a simple summer dress. Play with your colourway and yarn weights to create a unique collar for every mood and every outfit!

YARN WEIGHT
DK (light worsted)

HOOK SIZE
4mm/US size G-6
(or to match tension)

TENSION
One single pentagon motif = 11.5cm (4½in) from centre of flat edge to point

SIZE
One size, widest point across shoulders = 40cm (15¾in)

SAMPLE
Sample shown in DK yarn in a mix of wool and acrylic. Outer rounds and edging worked in a light colour base yarn with 3 contrast colours for the inners of shapes. Shapes joined with double crochet join.

APPROXIMATE METERAGE
Total = 140m (154yd)
Base colour = 70m (77yd)
Contrasting colours = 70m (77yd)

TOTAL SHAPES
Six pentagons

6

COLLAR
Step by Step Pattern Guide

COLLAR JOIN

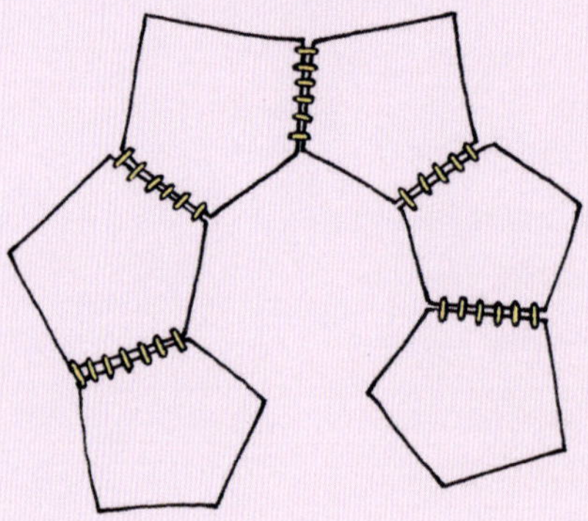

COLLAR BORDER ROUND

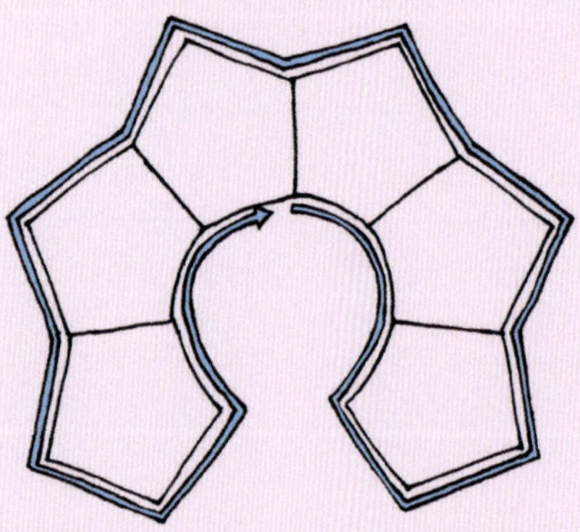

EDGING AND TIES

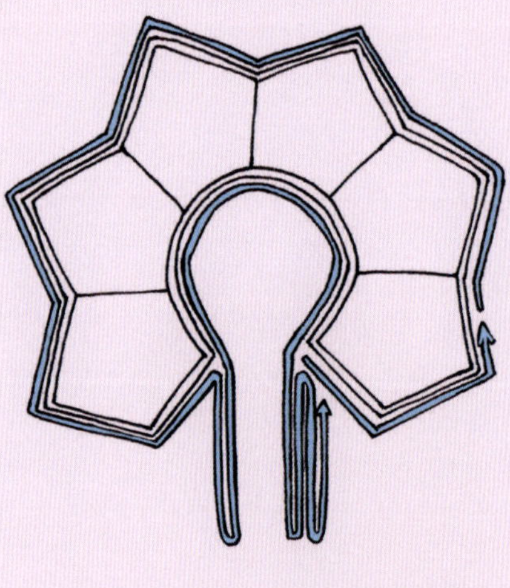

Getting Started

SHAPES

Make six pentagons.

The shapes in this project can be joined in any style, so fasten off all full-sized shapes with the length of tail determined by the join you wish to use (see pages 76–81).

COLOURWAY

Mix the colour order of the contrast colour rounds for each pentagon.

- Round 1: contrast colour 1
- Round 2: contrast colour 2
- Round 3: contrast colour 3
- Round 4: base colour

Instructions

JOINING

Collar Join

A Use your long tails to join the pentagons in your preferred joining method. Join the edges to create a U-shape.

Collar Border Round

A Working on the right side of your work, using base colour, join into the corner chain space to the right of centre (left space if left-handed).

B Chain 3.

C Treble 2 together over join, working the first half of the stitch in the same chain space and second half in next chain space, treble into chain space to complete cluster over join.

D Continue round across the entire collar by following the instructions for granny stitch extension rounds (see page 88). Work over all shape joins with the dipped joins technique to keep narrowing the neck shaping.

E Join with a slip stitch into the third chain at the start of the round to complete round.

Edging and Ties

A Continuing in base colour, chain 1.

B Work 1 double crochet into each stitch up to first corner chain space.

C Double crochet into corner chain space.

D Chain 41 stitches.

E Miss first stitch.

F Double crochet along chain, working into the back bump across 40 stitches.

G Double crochet into the next 2 stitches on the collar to anchor.

H If you wish to make a thicker style tie, turn work and double crochet back across the tie. If you want a thinner cord, skip this and the next two steps.

I Chain 1.

J Turn, double crochet 40 stitches back to collar.

K Continue using the double crochet round technique (see page 86) to work across the pointed collar edge, until you reach 2 stitches (1 stitch if making skinnier tie) before the last corner.

L Chain 41 stitches.

M Miss 1 stitch.

N Double crochet along chain, working into the back bump across 40 stitches.

O Double crochet into the next 2 stitches on the collar to anchor.

P If you wish to make a thicker style tie, turn work and double crochet back across the tie. If you want a thinner cord, skip this and the next two steps.

Q Chain 1.

R Turn, double crochet 40 stitches back to collar.

S Double crochet in corner stitch and work across up to first stitch of the round.

T Slip stitch into first stitch to complete the round.

U Fasten off.

FINISHING

A Sew in any remaining yarn ends.

B Block piece to finish.

TOP TIP

Size your yarn up to make the perfect statement collar for a denim jacket. If you are using a super chunky (super bulky) yarn, reduce the number of pentagons by one or two. Omit the ties and add a button to the inside of one corner. To attach, place the top denim jacket button through one corner chain space of the collar, and use the button on the inside corner of the collar to attach to the top button hole of the jacket.

Perfect Pouch

The handiest mini pouch bag you can make! This mini bag is the perfect size for your phone or a pair of sunglasses, and it has a pocket to fit your bank card. Its strap works to make it self-fastening, so your goodies won't fall out! You can make it with a long strap to work as a cross-body pouch or a short strap to attach to another bag as a practical bag charm.

YARN WEIGHT
DK (light worsted)

HOOK SIZE
4mm/US size G-6
(or to match tension)

TENSION
One single square motif = 9 x 9cm (3½ x 3½in)

SIZE
One pouch size with two strap lengths.
Pouch size = 19 x 9 cm (7½ x 3½in)
Long strap drop length = 50cm (19¾in)
Short strap drop length = 15cm (6in)

SAMPLES
Two design variations are shown (both worked in cotton DK and using double crochet join):

Variation 1: Graphic colour block and half 'n' half squares with a long strap, in contrast colours and black join
Variation 2: 2 colour Granny stripe with a short strap.

APPROXIMATE METERAGE
Total: 100m (110yd)

TOTAL SHAPES
Five squares.

5

TOP TIP

This project works well in cotton yarn as it is durable and has the strength needed for a thin strap, so it can take lots of wear.

PERFECT POUCH

Step by Step Pattern Guide

POUCH BAG BODY

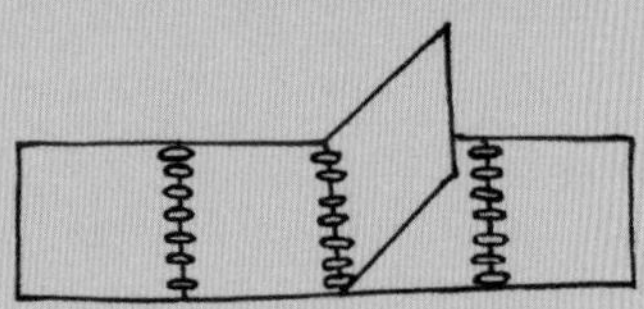

POUCH BAG POCKET EDGE

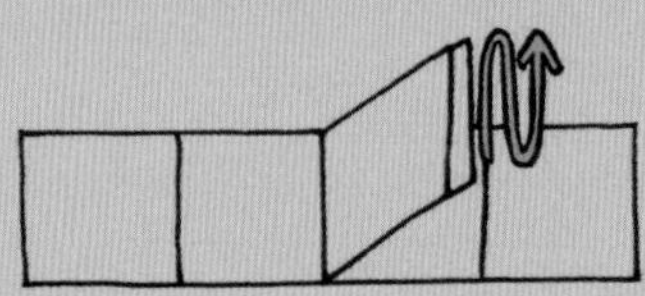

POUCH BAG JOIN

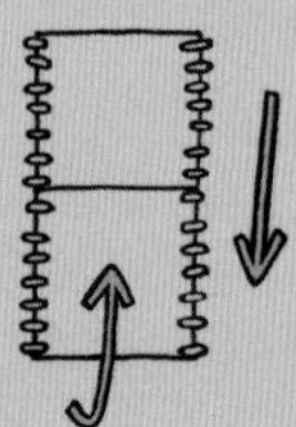

POUCH EDGING AND STRAP

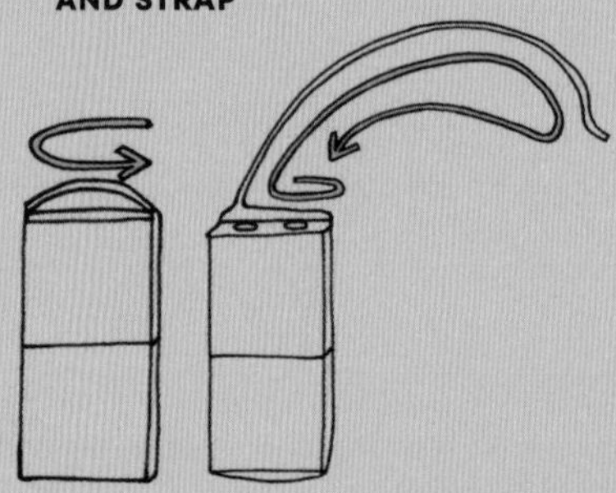

POUCH FASTENING AND FINISHING

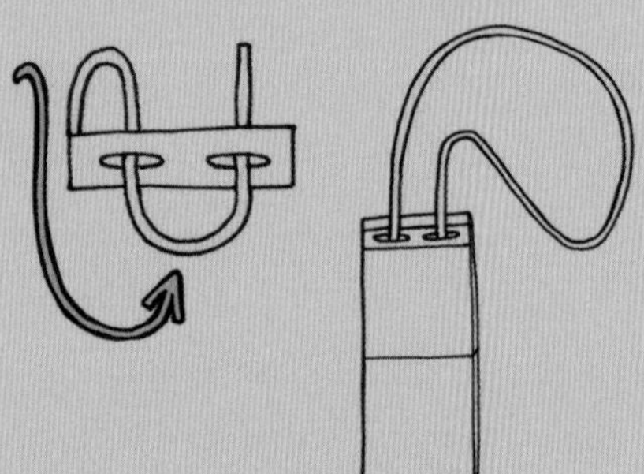

Getting Started

SHAPES

Make five squares: these could be the standard square or half 'n' half squares, depending on your chosen design. This project works best with a solid join – I recommend the double crochet join (see page 81) for a sturdy bag. If you are joining your standard squares, do so with the same colour as the last round of the square. Fasten off all squares with the length of tail determined by the join you wish to use (see pages 76–81).

COLOURWAY

Of your five squares, make sure two are the same colourway – these two matching squares will become the pocket. If you are working the two-colour stripe version, use the travel-up colour technique (see page 93).

Instructions

JOINING

Pouch Bag Body

A Using your joining yarn colour, or long yarn tails, double crochet join your squares into a strip of 4, with 1 double-layer square.

B On the third square across, create your pocket edge join. For this you need 2 squares facing the same way up, stacked on top of each other and joined into the strip as if they were 1 square. This will mean working through 3 layers at once.

C Once you have joined the thicker 3-layer seam, remember to go back to working just the bottom layer into your join for the last join of the row.
D You will finish with a strip of 4 with a flap on the 3rd square across, joined at the middle of the strip.

Pocket Edging

Using the same colour yarn you wish to use for your straps, edge the top of the flap.

Row 1:

A Starting with the yarn on your hook, join in with a double crochet join in the top corner chain space.
B Double crochet into the top of each stitch along one side of the square.

Row 2:

A Turn, chain 1.
B Double crochet into each stitch across.

Row 3:

A Turn.
B Slip stitch into each stitch along row. Work this stitch loosely, do not pull too tight.
C After last stitch, fasten off the yarn.

Pouch Side Joins

A Fold your bag strip in half with right sides together, wrong sides facing out.
B Join the pouch sides using your joining colour.
C Start with the yarn on your hook at the bottom of the bag. Work through the corner chain spaces on the fold, joining with a double crochet join. Because this section includes the pocket you will be working through 3 layers.
D Double crochet through each stitch along the first square block, working through the 3 layers to join.
E Double crochet through the squares' join stitch, through the first row of double crochet edging in your middle layer and into the opposite join stitch.
F Work the next double crochet through the next corner chain space, through the 2nd row of double crochet edging in your middle layer and into the opposite corner chain space.
G Work the next double crochet through the next st, through the top slip stitch in your middle layer edging and into the opposite square stitch.
H Continue working 1 double crochet through each stitch, joining the 2 layers, until your reach the last corner chain space.
I Work your last double crochet stitch through the 2 corners.
J Fasten off.
K Repeat on the other edge.

Pouch Edging and Strap

Round 1:

A In your strap yarn colour, join in with a double crochet join through the side join stitch.
B Work 1 double crochet into each stitch all the way around the top of the pouch.
C Slip stitch into the first stitch to complete the round.
D You should have a round of 30 stitches.

Round 2:

A Chain 1.
B Double crochet 18 stitches.
C Chain 3.
D Miss 2.
E Double crochet 5.
F Chain 3.
G Miss 2.
H Double crochet 2 stitches to the end of round.
I Slip stitch into the first chain to complete the round.

Round 3:

A Chain 1.
B Double crochet 3 stitches.
C Chain for 100cm (39½in) for the long strap or 30cm (12in) for the short strap. You can also create a customised length, just chain as desired.
D Miss the first 2 stitches of the chain.
E Half treble into the back bump of each stitch along the chain until you reach the pouch's back edge.
F Double crochet into the next stitch of the pouch edge.
G Double crochet into each stitch till you reach the chain space.
H Work 2 double crochet over chain.
I Double crochet 4.
J Work 2 double crochet over chain space.
K Double crochet back to start of round.
L Slip stitch into the first chain to join the round.

Row 4:

A Take the strap and thread it through the first chain space opposite, moving from the inside to the outside. Take the strap across the front of the pouch and back through the second chain space, from the outside to the inside of the pouch.
B Slip stitch into the top of the stitches of the last round for 10 stitches, work over where you first started the strap across the top edge.
C Making sure the strap isn't twisted, secure it by slip stitching through the pouch edge and strap end as 2 layers for the next 3 slip stitches.
D Slip stitch into the next 2 stitches.
E Fasten off.

FINISHING

Sew in any remaining yarn ends.

Neckerchief Scarf

The perfect mini scarf worked two ways for all seasons. Make this piece in a lightweight DK yarn for a super-cute neckerchief, great to give that spring shirt a touch of hand-crafted style. Or size up to Aran weight yarn to produce a winter warmer; the double wrap scarf style is perfect for those blustery days or when you're on your bike as its clever pull through fastening will keep it in place!

YARN WEIGHT
DK (light worsted) for neckerchief
Aran (worsted) for scarf

HOOK SIZE
4mm/US size G-6 for DK
(or to match tension)
5mm/US size H-8 for Aran
(or to match tension)

TENSION
One single square motif made in DK yarn = 9 x 9 cm (3½ x 3½in)
One single square motif made in Aran yarn = 11 x 11 cm (4¼ x 4¼in)

SIZE
Neckerchief length = 78cm (30¾in)
Scarf length = 140cm (55in)

SAMPLES
Two design variations are shown:

Variation 1: Neckerchief/joined with mattress stitch/worked in a DK cotton blend using the two-colour travel-up technique (see page 73).

Variation 2: Scarf/joined with double crochet/worked in an Aran wool yarn with colour changing each round and a base colour final round, using the weave-as-you-go colour technique (see page 74).

APPROXIMATE METERAGE
Total neckerchief: 120m (131yd)
Total scarf: (230m (252yd)

TOTAL SHAPES
Neckerchief: Four squares, three mini squares and two pentagons

4 3 2

Scarf: Eight squares, three mini squares and two pentagons

8 3 2

NECKERCHIEF SCARF

Step by Step Pattern Guide

NECK SQUARES

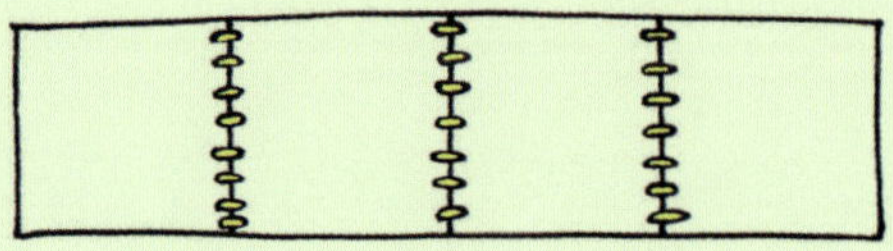

OR

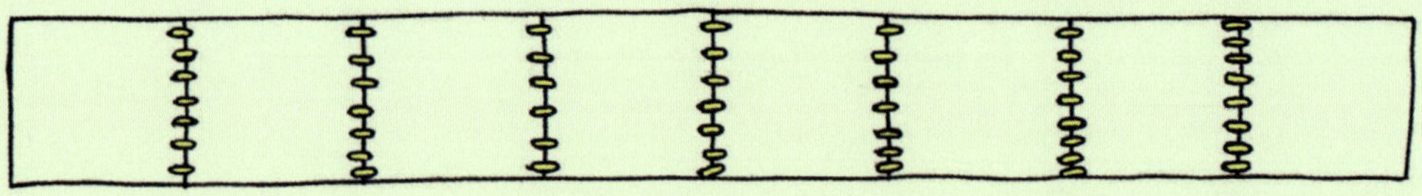

MINI SQUARES

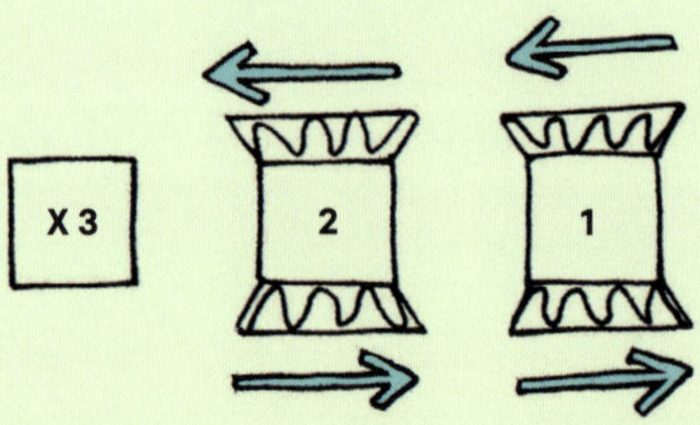

END JOINS

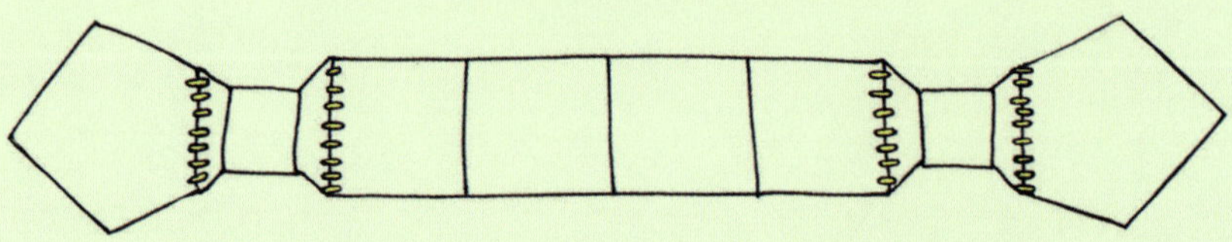

EDGING

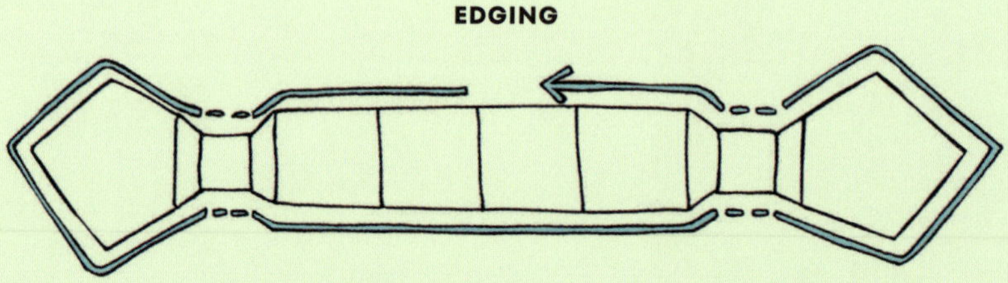

Getting Started

SHAPES

Make four squares for a neckerchief (eight for a double-wrap scarf), two pentagons and three three-round mini squares. To make the mini squares, follow the square pattern but stop at round 3. This project works best with a solid join, so use the double crochet join (see page 81) or either of the sewn joins (see pages 79–81). Fasten off all full-sized shapes with the length of tail determined by the join you wish to use.

VARIATION 1 (NECKERCHIEF) COLOURWAY

Make two squares in following colour order:

- Round 1: colour 1 (use travel-up colour technique, see page 73)
- Round 2: colour 2
- Round 3: colour 1
- Round 4: colour 2

Make the remaining two squares, three mini squares and two pentagons following the opposite colour order.

VARIATION 2 (SCARF) COLOURWAY

Make all full-sized shapes in following colour order:

- Round 1: colour 1 (the weave-as-you-go colour change works well here, see page 74)
- Round 2: colour 2
- Round 3: colour 3
- Round 4: base colour

Instructions

JOINING

Neck Squares

A Use your long tails to join your shapes using your preferred closed joining method. Join the neck squares together in a strip.

Mini Squares

A Take 2 of your mini squares and place them back-to-back with wrong sides together.
B Using the same colour as the final round, join the squares together with a slip stitch through any corner space, working through both layers.
C Chain 3, treble 3 times into the same corner.
D Work 1 cluster into each of the next 2 spaces working through both layers.
E Work 4 trebles into the corner chain space working through both layers.
F Fasten off leaving a long tail to join with.
G Repeat this process on the opposite edge to create a shape with 2 closed edges and an opening to pull the scarf through.
H Repeat this process – without the need to work through 2 layers – on the remaining single square, to make a single-layer version.
I Join these to either end of your joined neck squares using your preferred joining method.

End Joins

A Join the pentagons to each end of your scarf/neckerchief using your preferred joining method.

FINISHING

Optional Edging

Add a finishing touch by working a round of double crochet around the edge (see page 86). This works best on styles that have shapes ending in the same base colour. To avoid adding bulk over the mini squares, when you reach this section, work a slip stitch through the stitches on the mini squares. Remember to only work in the top layer of the two-layer square.

A Sew in any remaining yarn ends.
B Block piece to finish.

TOP TIP

This design can also be teamed with the bonnet (see page 152) to make a hood/balaclava design. Follow the neckerchief style, working in an Aran weight yarn using the same hook size as for the bonnet.

Cozy Cowboy Slipper Socks

A fun, silly slipper to keep those toes warm in Dolly Parton style! The Cozy Cowboy Slipper Socks use a mixture of squares and hexagons to create an ankle-height wool booty. Crocheted with a tight tension for a dense fabric, you could even work in wool, which you could felt slightly to make your sock sturdier.

YARN WEIGHT
Aran (worsted)

HOOK SIZE
4mm/US size G-6 (or to match tension) = Size 1

4.5mm/US size 7 (or to match tension) = Size 2

5mm/US size H-8 (or to match tension) = Size 3

TENSION
One single square motif =
Size 1 = 9 x 9cm (3½ x 3½in)
Size 2 = 9.5 x 9.5cm (3¾ x 3¾in)
Size 3 = 10.5 x 10.5cm (4 x 4in)

SIZE
Size 1 = approximately 24cm (9½in) foot length, UK size 3–5 shoe size.

Size 2 = approximately 26cm (10¼in) foot length, UK size 6–8 shoe size.

Size 3 = approximately 30cm (11¾in) foot length, UK size 9–12 shoe size.

SAMPLES
Three design variations are shown:
Variation 1:
Granny stripe colourway
Variation 2:
Cowboy boot style 2 colours
Variation 3:
Cowboy boot style 3 colours

APPROXIMATE METERAGE
Total meterage is dependent on the size made, see chart on page 132.

TOTAL SHAPES
Twelve squares and four hexagons

12 4

COZY COWBOY SLIPPER SOCKS

Step by Step Pattern Guide

SOLE JOIN

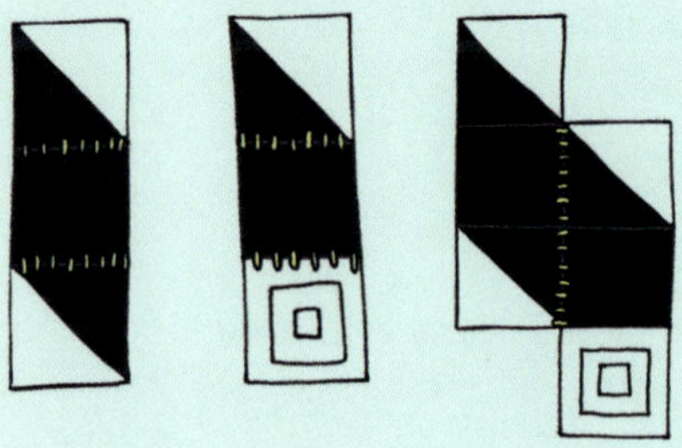

FOOT JOIN

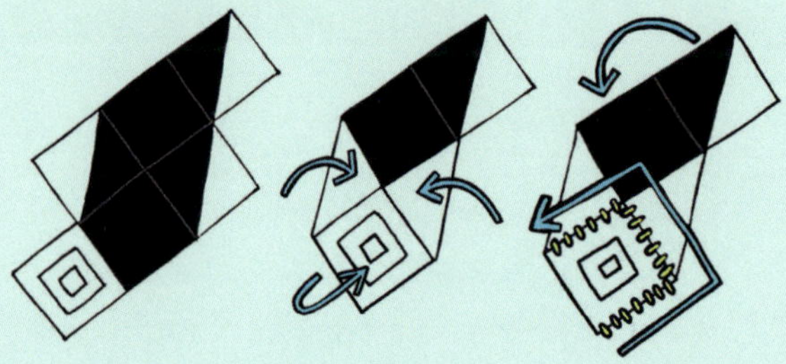

FOOT

ANKLE

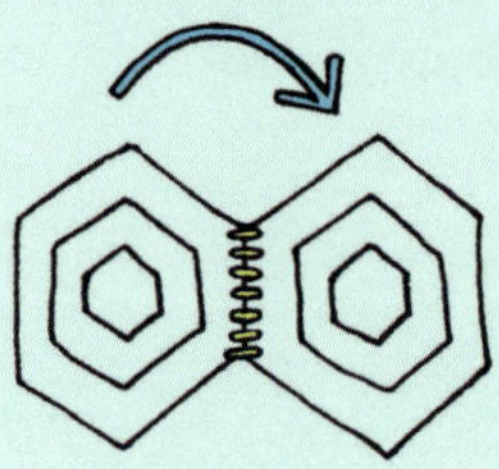

BOOT JOIN

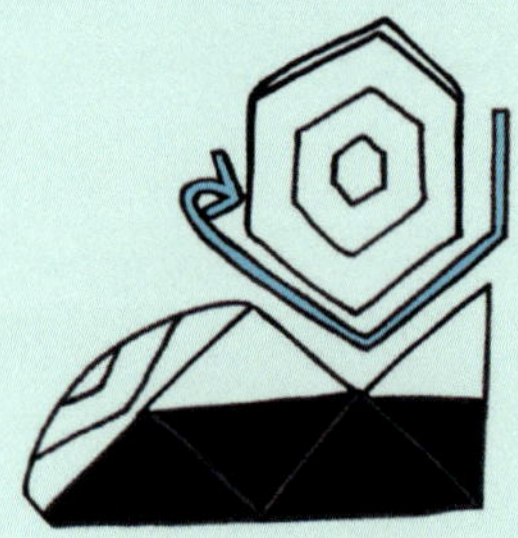

TRIM

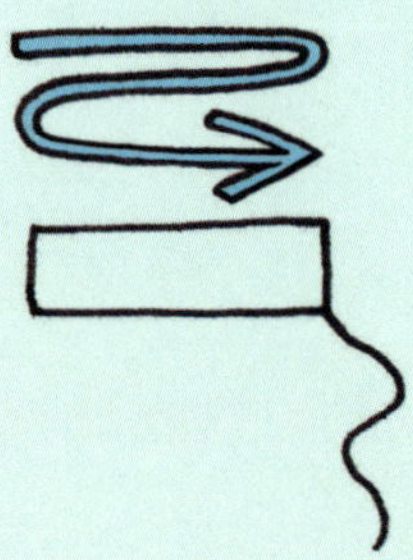

EDGING

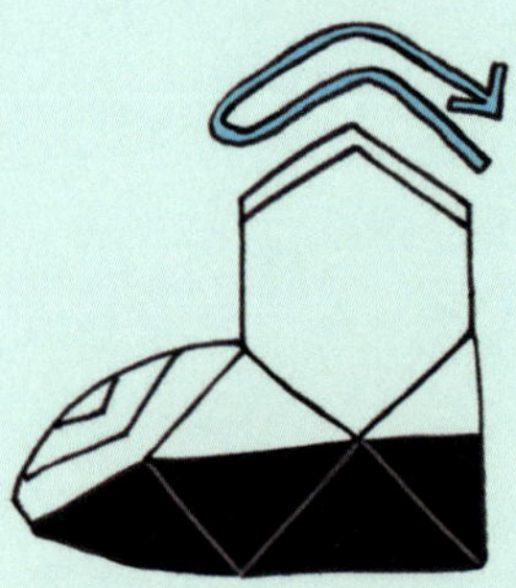

FINISHING

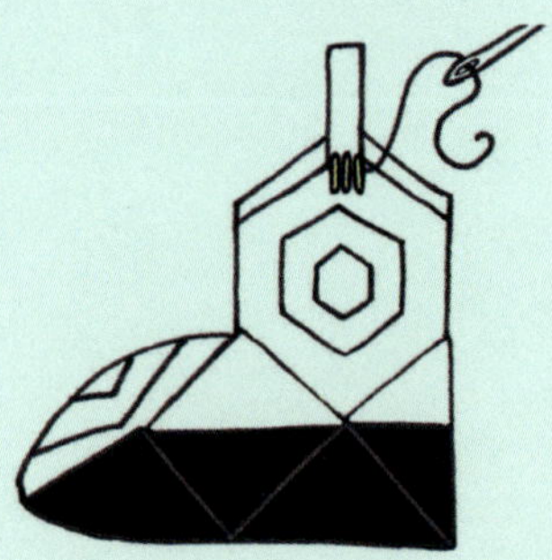

Getting Started

SHAPES

For all versions make 12 squares. If working version 1 follow colourway for all shapes. If making version 2 or 3 in the cowboy style make four in the block base colour, six half 'n' half with the base colour and colour 1, and make two patterned squares and four hexagons following the colourway order. Fasten off all squares with the length of tail determined by the join you wish to use (see pages 76–81).

COLOURWAY

- Round 1: base colour (use travel-up colour technique, see page 73)
- Round 2: contrast colour 1
- Round 3: base colour
- Round 4: contrast colour 2

Instructions

JOINING

Follow the specific joining order for versions 2 and 3. For version 1, just follow the squares general layout. Using the base colour make up the slipper and create the trim. Divide the shapes into two lots to make two socks. Each sock requires: two block base colour squares, three half 'n' half squares, one patterned square and two patterned hexagons. Follow the instructions to make one sock, then repeat to make the second sock.

Sole and Foot join

A Create 2 strips of 3 squares, each using the long tail to double crochet join the edges. Follow the diagram for the colour pattern and square order.

B Using your joining colour, join the 2 strips of 3 squares together in the order shown in the diagram. Four squares should meet in the centre. Start with the yarn on your hook and work on the wrong side (inside the sock) using the double crochet join (see page 81).

C With the right side facing up, follow the diagram to fold in the edges so that the wrong side faces out. You can hold your squares in place with stitch markers.

D Following the diagram, join along three edges to create the toe of your slipper.

E Join in yarn with a double crochet in the corner chain space of the toe. Work into each stitch along the first to the next corner.

F Turn to work along the 2nd edge, work back into the corner chain space of the toe square and along the edge until next corner chain space, double crochet through corners, chain 1.

G Double crochet back through the corner, and now join along 3rd edge.

H Fasten off after working into the last corner chain space.

I Fold in the ankle square and join the edge shown to complete the foot section of your slipper. When folded flat this will be a diamond shape.

Ankle and Boot join

A Using your joining colour and working on the wrong side, join the hexagons together with a double crochet join (see page 81).

B The join just made will be positioned at the front of your slipper. Have the foot section of your boot inside out and use stitch markers to hold the hexagons in place on top of it.

C Join in your yarn with a double crochet join at the centre-top back chain space and work along the back seam of the hexagon to create the ankle section.

D Continue to attach the ankle section to the foot. Double crochet through each stitch along the edges. When you reach a hexagon corner and it meets 3 square corners, make sure you work through the hexagon corner 3 times with a double crochet, joining with one square corner each time.

E Continue joining with double crochet until you reach the last stitch at the back of the sock.

F Fasten off.

Ankle Edging

A Work the edging along the open edge of the hexagons. Turn the sock the right way out with the join seams on the inside.

B Join in with a slip stitch at the centre back. Chain 1, double crochet into each stitch.

C At the outward pointing corners (double crochet, chain 1, double crochet) in chain space.

D Join with a slip stitch into the first chain at the start of the round to complete round.

E Fasten off and weave in any loose ends.

Ankle Loops
Foundation Chain

A Using the base colour, chain 21.

Row 1:

A Miss first stitch.

B Double crochet into each back bump of the chain, giving you 20 sts.

Row 2:

A Chain 1.

B Double crochet across working into each stitch.

Row 3:

A Repeat Row 2. Fasten off leaving a 20cm (8in) tail.

Attach:

Attach the ankle loop using a tapestry needle. Fold the loop in half and weave it through the gap in the second round of your hexagon at the top side point of hexagon. Use the yarn tail to sew ends together to create a loop. Repeat to create a loop on the opposite side of the ankle.

TOP TIPS

To get the perfect fit for your foot, use real wool and hand wash in warm soapy water to shrink or stretch to foot size. Do this by hand and not in the washing machine to control the shrinkage. If you want to felt your make to get a sturdier slipper sock, work a larger size initially and shrink to fit.

Size down your yarn to DK weight and use a 3mm (US size C-2 or D-3) hook for a kids' size sock.

SIZE	MEASUREMENTS		APPROXIMATE METERAGE (YDS)		
	SHOE SIZE UK SIZE	FOOT LENGTH IN CM (IN)	TOTAL	SHAPES TOTAL	CONTRAST JOIN & TRIM
1	3–5	24cm (9½in)	285 (312)	235 (257)	55 (61)
2	6–8	26cm (10¼in)	295 (323)	240 (263)	60 (66)
3	9–12	30cm (11¾in)	320 (350)	260 (285)	65 (72)

TOP TIPS

Size up from a floor cushion to a larger pouffe by doubling up the hexagon row around the centre!

This project also works as great hidden yarn storage. Disguise your WIP pile and yarn stash by using it as filling! Use a small duvet cover or a few pillowcases as covers and fill them with yarn, this can then be used to stuff the floor cushion.

Floor Cushion Cozy

Dress up your living room in crochet goodness. The Floor Cushion Cozy is the perfect accompaniment to your sofa style and great to put your feet up on while you crochet! This project makes use of three of the shapes to get its form and is worked up in chunky yarn. Cotton tape yarn gives this project a clean and crisp look and the bottom has a drawstring so the cover can easily be taken off and washed. This project needs an inner pad fill it out – kids' beanbags or floor cushions are ideal for this.

YARN WEIGHT
Chunky (bulky)

HOOK SIZE
8mm/US size L-11
(or to match tension)

TENSION
One hexagon, flat edge to flat edge = 20cm (8in)

SIZE
One size:
Floor cushion size = 60 x 25cm (24 x 9¾in)

SAMPLE
Worked in chunky cotton ribbon yarn, with ecru base colour and 5 contrast colours. Joined using both whip stitch and double crochet join.

APPROXIMATE METERAGE
Total: 925m (1012yd)
Base colour: 405m (443yd)
Contrasting colours:
520m (569yd)
See table on page 138 for each contrast colour amount.

TOTAL SHAPES
One octagon
16 pentagons
Eight hexagons

1 16 8

FLOOR CUSHION COZY

Step by Step Pattern Guide

PENTAGON JOINS

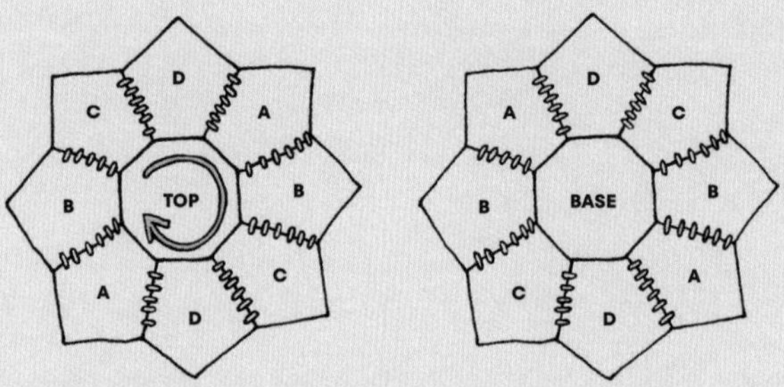

OCTAGON TOP JOIN

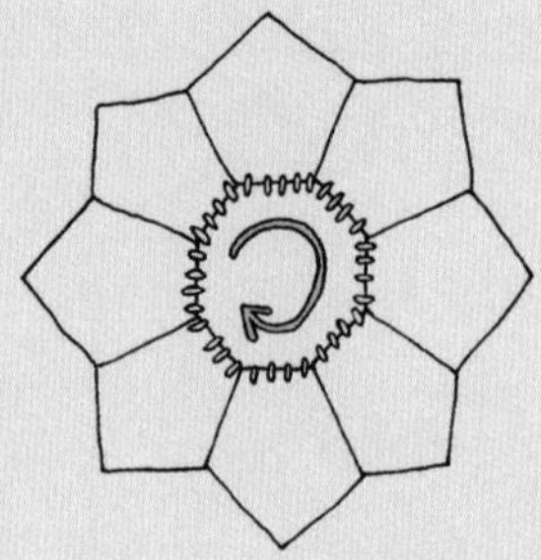

HEXAGON JOINS

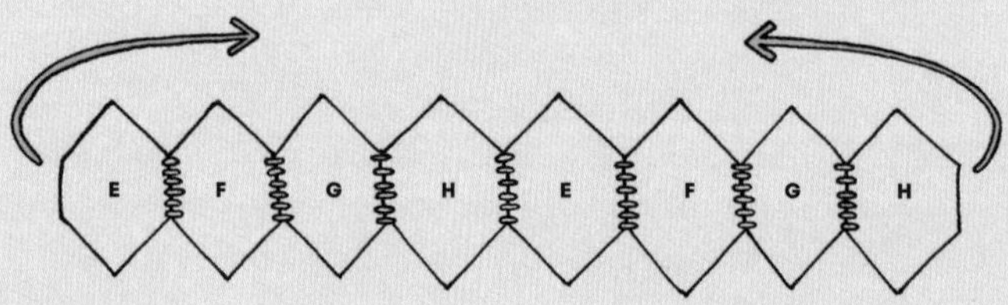

SIDE JOIN

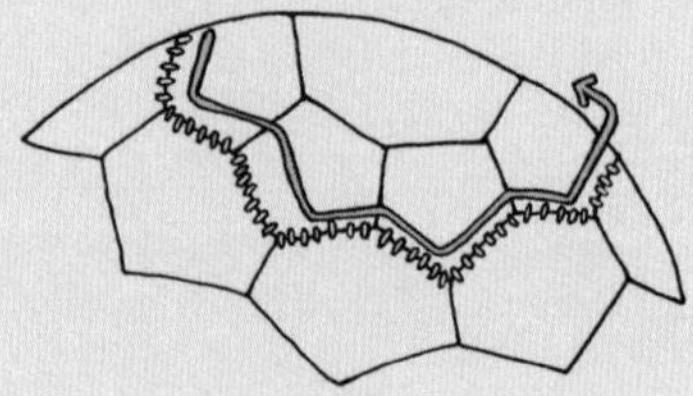

BASE JOIN

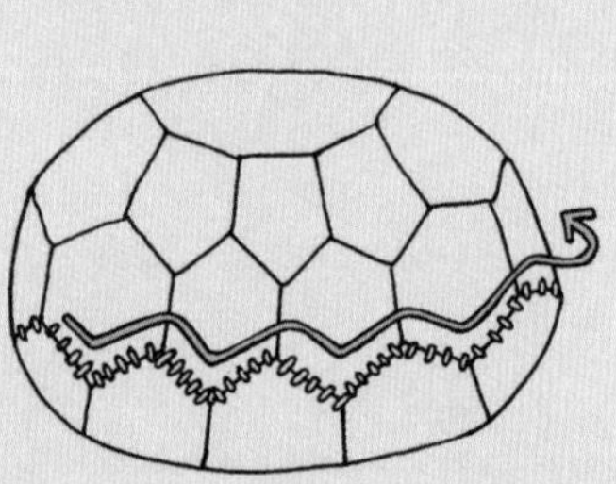

BASE MESH FILL

BASE DRAWSTRING

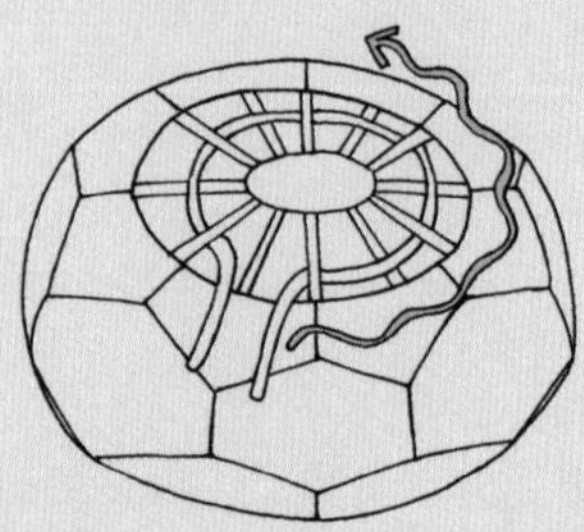

Getting Started

SHAPES

Make one octagon. 16 pentagons – four in each colourway with a whip stitch long-tail fasten off (see page 78); and eight hexagons – two in each colourway with a whip stitch long-tail fasten off. If you are making the larger pouffe variation, double the number of hexagons to add a second line.

For this project you will also need an inner pad to stuff your floor cushion or pouffe. Kids' beanbags or floor cushions work well for this. The pad I used for the floor cushion was 70 x 20cm (27½ x 8in) in size.

COLOURWAY

There is a colour mix of four contrast colours and a base colour. Following the order in the chart on page 138 will help you use your contrast colours evenly.

Instructions

JOINING

Pentagon Joins

A Create both your top and base by joining your pentagons together in 2 rings.

B Use your long tail from fastening off to whip stitch one edge of each of your pentagons together to form a ring.

C Join the pieces together following the whip stitch technique on page 78. Follow the colour order in the diagram.

D You should now have 2 pentagon rings with mirrored colour orders.

Cozy Top

A With your base colour and working on the wrong side, use a double crochet join to attach the top octagon.

B Use stitch markers to hold the octagon in place, matching up the corner points with the pentagons.

C Using the double crochet joining method (see page 81), start in any octagon corner chain space and join with a double crochet into the pentagon corner.

D Work your join over the tail of the yarn you have added or any other tails to trap your yarn ends, this saves you from sewing them in at the end.

E Double crochet through both layers up to the next octagon corner.

F In the corner, work one double crochet through the octagon corner and the corner of the pentagon that you have worked across.

G Work back into the same octagon corner with a double crochet, now joining into the next pentagon in your pattern.

H Repeat steps E to F until you have worked all the way round the octagon.

I Work your final double crochet into the corner you started joining in, along with your final pentagon corner.

J Fasten off.

Hexagon Joins

A Use a tapestry needle to weave your long tail (from fastening off) through the tops of the stitches to the nearest corner of a hexagon.

B Use your long-tail fasten off to whip stitch one edge of each of your hexagons together to form a ring.

C Join the pieces together following the whip stitch technique on page 78. Follow the colour order in the diagram.

Side Join and Base Join

A With your base colour, working on the wrong side (inside the cushion cozy), use a double crochet join to attach the top to the side panel.

B Use stitch markers to hold the shapes in place, matching up the corner points.

C Using the double crochet join method (see page 81) start in any hexagon point corner chain space and join with a double crochet into the pentagon corner.

D Work your join over the tail of the yarn you have added, or any other tails, to trap your yarn ends, this saves you from sewing them in at the end.

E Double crochet through both layers up to the next hexagon corner chain space.

F In the corner, work 1 double crochet through hexagon corner and the pentagon point chain space that you have worked across.

G Work into the next hexagon corner chain space and then back into the same pentagon point chain space, joining with a double crochet.

H Work double crochet along the edge until you reach the next hexagon point chain space.

I Double crochet through the hexagon point chain space and into the pentagon point chain space.

J Double crochet through the same hexagon point chain space and into the next pentagon corner chain space.

K Repeat steps E to J until you have worked all the way round your side join.
L Fasten off.
M Line up your base panel so that the colours mirror the top panel. Secure with stitch markers to hold the panel in place and join in the same way as for the top panel, repeating steps B to L to attach the base panel.

Base Mesh Fill

Round 1:

A Using your base colour, join in with a slip stitch between any cluster space on the bottom inside (wrong side) edge.
B Chain 3, treble 2 into the same space to make your first cluster.
C Work one cluster into each gap between clusters up to corner chain space.
D In corner chain space, work 1 treble.
E In the same space, reduce the stitches by working treble 2 together over the join. Work the first part of the first treble in the same space and work the second half of the stitch in the next corner chain space, close the stitch.
F Work 1 treble in the second corner chain space. This creates 1 cluster that is worked over the 2 corners, reducing your stitches.
G Repeat steps C to F until you have worked around the base.

Round 2:

A Slip stitch into a space between clusters.
B Chain 6.
C Double treble into next space between clusters.
D Chain 2, double treble into next space.
E Repeat step D until you have worked around the entire round.
F Join into the 4th chain at the start of the round with a slip stitch.

Round 3:

A Slip stitch into a space between clusters.
B Chain 6.
C Double treble into next chain space.
D Chain 2, double treble into next space.
E Repeat step D until you have worked around the entire round.
F Join into the 4th chain at the start of the round with a slip stitch.
G Fasten off.

Drawstring

A Make a chain approx. 1m (39½in) long. Fasten off.
B Weave the chain cord between stitches of round 3 to create a drawstring.

Finishing

A Sew in any remaining yarn ends.
B Add the inner cushion pad then draw up the drawstring to close the hole and tie in a bow to secure.

	A	B	C	D	E	F	G	H	Octagon
Round 1	Colour 5	Colour 3	Colour 4	Colour 3	Colour 1	Colour 2	Colour 3	Colour 4	Colour 1
Round 2	Colour 4	Colour 2	Colour 5	Colour 1	Colour 3	Colour 5	Colour 4	Colour 2	Colour 2
Round 3	Colour 3	Colour 1	Colour 3	Colour 2	Colour 2	Colour 4	Colour 1	Colour 5	Colour 3
Round 4	Base Colour	Base Colour	Base Colour	Base Colour	Base Colour	Base Colour	Base Colour	Base Colour	Colour 4
Round 5	–	–	–	–	–	–	–	–	Base Colour

	Base Color	Colour 1	Colour 2	Colour 3	Colour 4	Colour 5
Meterage (yd)	405 (443)	95 (104)	120 (131)	125 (137)	100 (109)	80 (88)
Total Meterage (yd)	925 (1012)					

Simple Squares Shopper

This versatile day-to-night bag is perfect as a first project! You can adjust where you knot its handy tie straps, taking it from cross-body shopper to big-bowed handbag. Its chunky yarn and simple construction make it the perfect quick, lazy day make. It's also fun to play around with different yarns for this design as a small change will make a big difference.

YARN WEIGHT
Chunky (bulky)

HOOK SIZE
7mm/US size K-10½ or L-11
(or to match tension)

TENSION
One four-round square =
14 x 14cm (5½ x 5½in)

SIZE
One size = 45cm (17¾in) wide
x 45cm (17¾in) long

SAMPLES
Two design variations are shown:

Variation 1:
Alternate stripes in chenille yarn using the colour travel-up technique for both colours and double crochet join
Variation 2:
Alternate stripes in chenille yarn with contrast colours in novelty eyelash yarn using the colour travel-up technique for base colour.

APPROXIMATE METERAGE
Total: 320m (350yd)
Colour 1: 200m (219yd)
Colour 2: 120m (131yd)

TOTAL SHAPES
Three extended squares

3

TOP TIP

You can make this bag bigger or smaller by playing around with the square size but also your yarn type. If switch your yarn, remember to also change your hook size to match it (see page 17).

SIMPLE SQUARES SHOPPER

Step by Step Pattern Guide

SQUARES JOIN

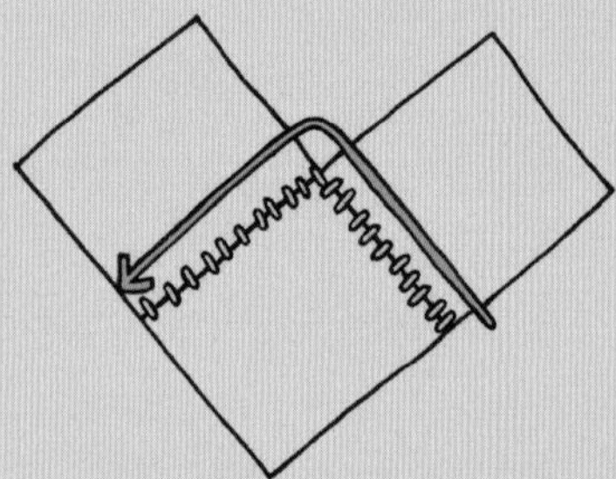

SQUARES FOLD

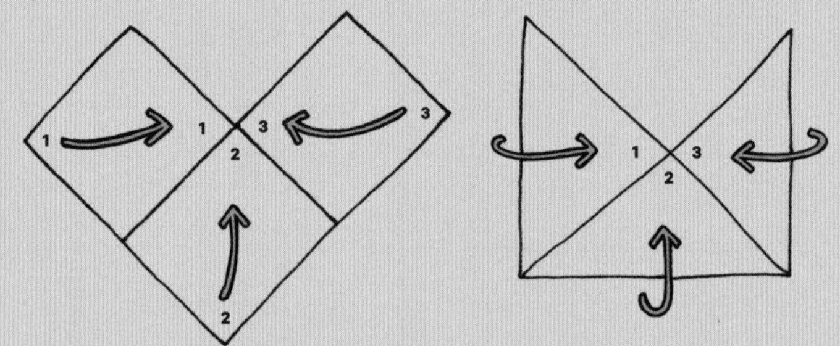

JOIN CONTINUED

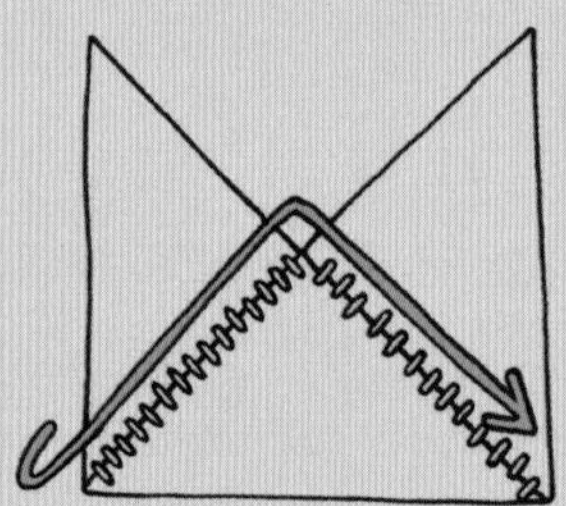

STRAP 1

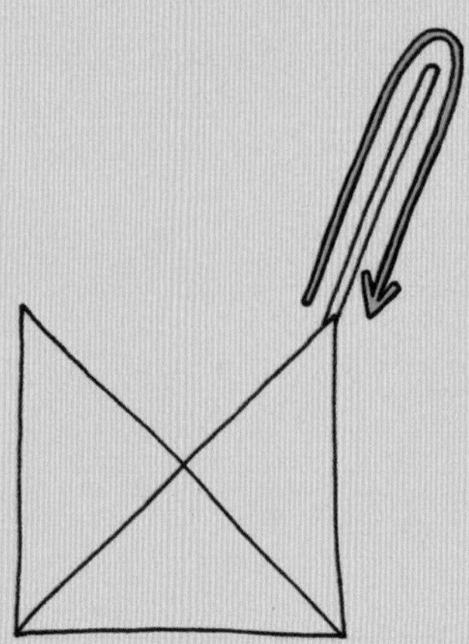

STRAP 2 AND TIES

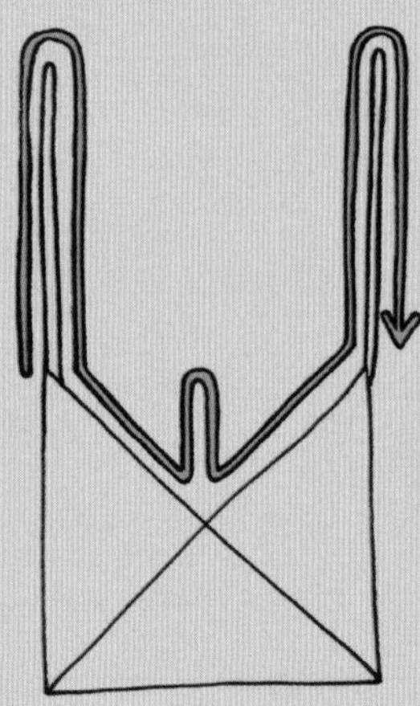

Getting Started

SHAPES

Make three extended squares with a total of nine rounds each. Fasten off the shapes with a short tail as you will be joining the squares with new yarn.

COLOURWAY

Worked in two colours: colour 1 is the first round colour for the squares, and the strap colour; colour 2 is the contrast colour – or colours if you are making the multicolour variation. Use the travel-up colour method (see page 93) to avoid having too many yarn ends.

Instructions

JOINING

Squares Join

A Lay out your 3 squares in an upside-down arrow shape.

B Start at the point where the edge square meets the bottom square and use colour 1 and the double crochet joining technique (see page 81) to join on the wrong side (inside the bag) of your squares.

C Join through the first corner chain space with a double crochet join.

D Work along the first edge up to the centre point.

E At the centre point, where the corner chain spaces meet, double crochet together.

F Double crochet through the middle square again but this time join with the corner of the next edge square.

G Double crochet join along the next square's edge.

H Leave the yarn live to continue after folding.

Squares Fold

Following the diagram, fold the squares to create the shape of the bag, use stitch markers to hold everything in place. Remember to fold your bag so that it is wrong side out for you to join.

Join Continued

A You can now continue joining the bag using a double crochet join.

B Double crochet back through both corner chain spaces.

C Join along the next edge to the central point.

D Work 1 double crochet through the corner chain space of both squares.

E Work a second double crochet through the middle square but now join with the next square.

F Work the double crochet join down the remaining edge until you reach the bottom corner.

G In the corner, double crochet through the corner chain space and fasten off.

Strap 1

A Using colour 1, join in with a double crochet join in one of the top corner chain spaces.

B Loosely chain 51 stitches.

C Turn and miss 1 stitch.

D Working through the back bump of the chain, double crochet 50.

E Anchor to the bag by double crocheting back into the corner chain space.

F Fasten off.

Strap 2 and Ties

A Repeat the instructions for Strap 1 on the other side of the bag but do not fasten off.

B Continue double crocheting along the top edge into each stitch until you reach the corner chain space.

C Double crochet into the corner chain space of the first square.

D Double crochet into the corner chain space of the middle square.

E Loosely chain 21 stitches.

F Turn and miss 1 stitch.

G Working through the back bump of the chain, slip stitch 20.

H Anchor to bag by double crocheting back into the middle corner chain space.

I Double crochet into the next corner chain space.

J Double crochet into each stitch until you reach the strap.

K Double crochet into each stitch along the strap. At the top of the strap, double crochet 3 into the same stitch to turn around the edge.

L Double crochet back down the other edge of the strap until you get to the body of the bag.

M Repeat steps B to L.

N Join with a slip stitch at the base of the strap and fasten off.

Finishing

A Sew in any remaining yarn ends.

B Block if needed.

Colour Lovin' Coatigan

The perfect cardigan/jacket hybrid, this coatigan is a cozy final layer that packs a punch. This make has a loose fit but you can also size up for a more oversized feel. Pick between two collar styles, classic or statement, whatever fits your style best! This garment is whipped up in a chunky yarn, go for something thick and cozy for a heavier weight garment or lighter and fluffy for a thinner layer – the choice is yours.

YARN WEIGHT
Chunky (bulky)

HOOK SIZE
7mm/US size K-10½ or L-11 (or to match tension)

TENSION
One four-round square = 16 x 16cm (6¼ x 6¼in)

SIZE
XS–5XL, see chart

EASE
30–40cm (11¾–15¾in) oversized fit

SAMPLES
Two design variations are shown:

Variation 1: Size L. Worked in velvety acrylic chenille yarn. A mix of nine colours with blue as the base colour and a statement pentagon collar. Sizing is adjusted by extending the squares and adding side extension rows. The sample is shown on a size S/M model for more relaxed, oversized fit.

Variation 2: Size S. Worked in chunky, fluffy lightweight acrylic mohair yarn using a colour changing yarn and brown as the base colour. This variation has a classic shape collar. Sample shown on size S and size M for fit guide if you are between sizes.

APPROXIMATE METERAGE
Total meterage will be determined by your chosen size, see chart on page 149.

TOTAL SHAPES
8 extended squares
12 mini squares
4 pentagons

8 12 4

COLOUR LOVIN' COATIGAN

Step by Step Pattern Guide

SQUARE SIDE SIZING ROWS

FRONT BODY JOIN AND TIE X 2

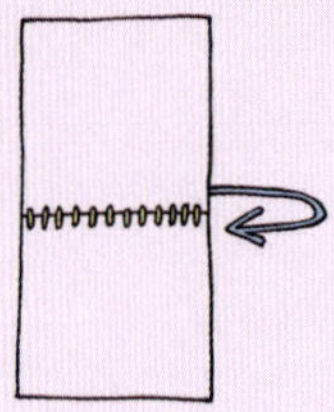

BACK PANEL JOIN

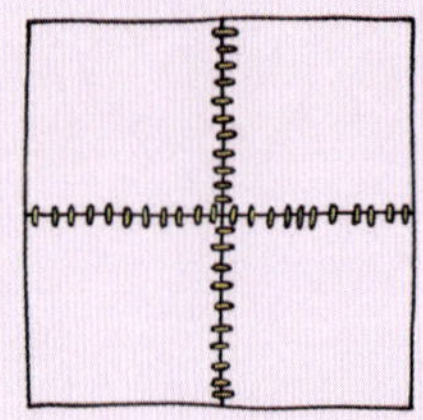

SLEEVE JOIN

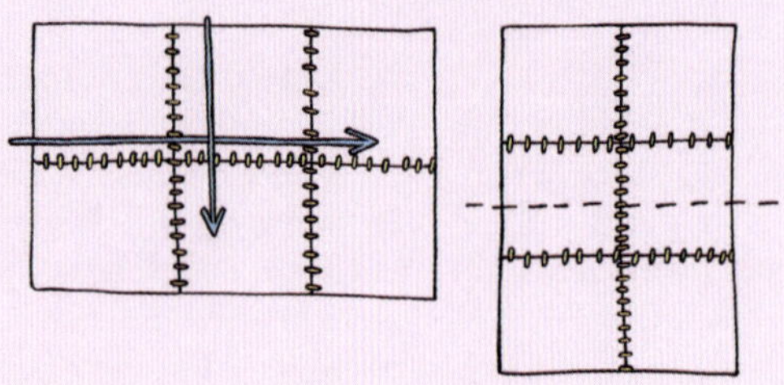

SIDE SEAM JOIN

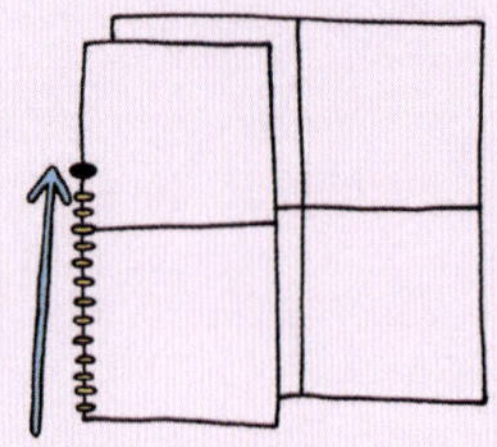

SLEEVE – BODY JOIN (1) AND TOP FRONT SLEEVE/SHOULDER ROWS (2)

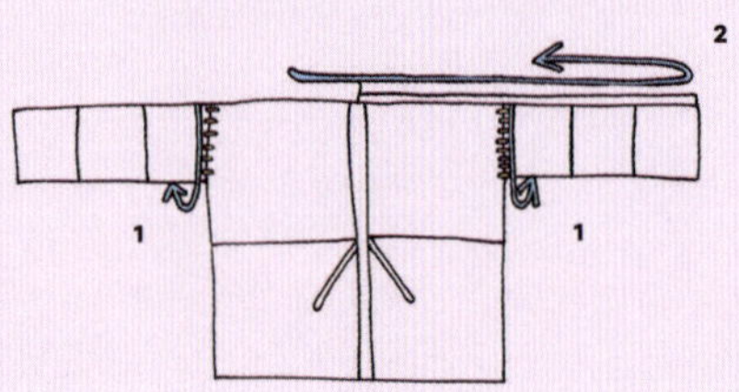

SLEEVE – TOP BACK ROWS

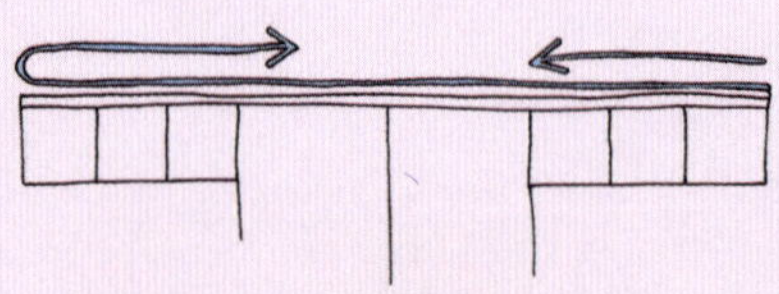

SLEEVE JOIN AND CUFF EXTENSION

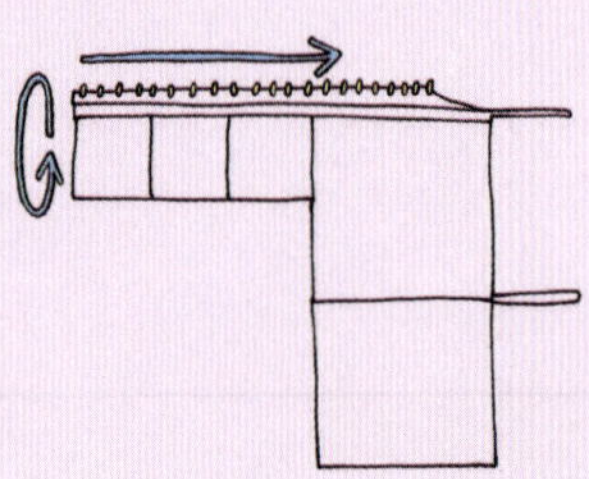

PENTAGON COLLAR

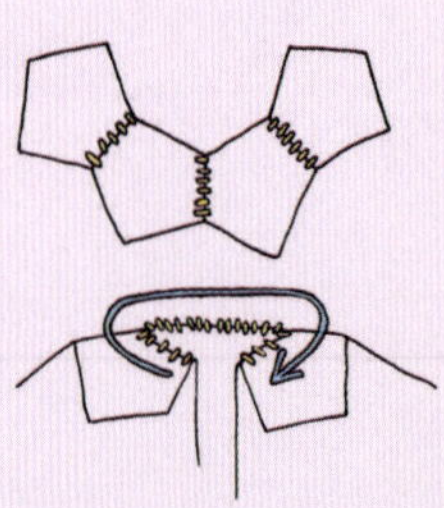

GRANNY ROWS COLLAR ALTERNATIVE

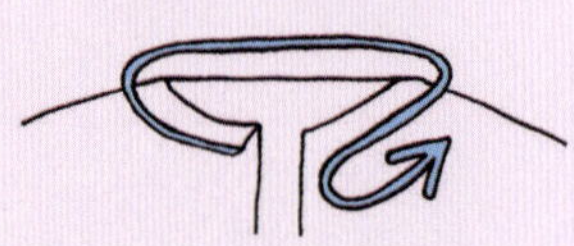

Getting Started

SHAPES

Make eight extended squares, working the number of rounds given for your chosen size in the chart on page 149. These could be enlarged traditional granny squares or even extended half 'n' half squares. For the sleeves, make the number of mini three-round squares specified in the chart. If you are making the statement collar, make four extra pentagons, and add a fifth extension round for sizes 3XL to 5XL. Fasten off with short tails as new yarn is used for joining. Join using the double crochet join (see page 81) worked on the right side as a detail.

COLOURWAY

Make your extended squares using a random mix of nine colours. Mix up the number of rounds you work in each colour to get a more unique stripe pattern. Use the weave-as-you-go method when changing colours (see page 74). Join most of your pieces using the double crochet join in your base colour on the right side of the work. Work the mini three-round sleeve squares and the pentagons in the colour orders listed below.

Square
Round 1: colour 1
Round 2: colour 1
Round 3: colour 2

Pentagon
Round 1: colour 1
Round 2: colour 1
Round 3: colour 2
Round 4: colour 2
Round 5: colour 3 (sizing optional)

Instructions

SQUARES

Body Squares

A Make the extended squares for the body, changing colours as desired.
B If you are adding sizing rows (see chart), extend using the granny stitch row technique on one side of your squares only (see page 89).

JOINING

Front Squares

A Lay out your squares to find your preferred colour balance, making sure extension rows are on the outer edges.
B Take the 2 pairs of front squares and place them wrong sides together.
C Using your base colour and working on the right side of the work, join working from the outside edge inwards using the double crochet join.
D When you reach the opposite corner space do not fasten off.
E Chain 26.
F Miss 1 stitch.
G Slip stitch through the back bump of 25 chains to create a tie.
H Fasten off when you have worked into the final chain.
I Sew in yarn ends.
J Repeat to create the second front panel.

Back Squares

A Using stitch markers, join the 4 back squares together.
B Using your base colour and the double crochet join, join the 4 back squares working on the right side of the work as a design detail.
C Work across the width and then join the centre back length.
D Fasten off.

Sleeve Squares

A Join your mini squares for the sleeves.
B Use the chart to check the sleeve dimensions and hold the squares together using stitch markers.
C Join using your base colour and the double crochet join, working on the right side of the crochet as a design detail.
D Work the longest join first to hold the squares in place, then work across the smaller joins.
E Repeat for the second sleeve.

Side Seams and Sleeve Seams

A At the outer side seams on the front and back body panels, count 11 stitches down for sleeves that are 1 square deep and 17 stitches down for sleeves that are 1.5 squares deep. This is your underarm point, mark your place with a stitch marker.
B Place the body panels together and, using your base colour and the double crochet join, join the side seam from the bottom up to the stitch marker, working on the right side of the work.
C Repeat on the other side.
D Once your side seams are joined, insert your sleeve.
E Open out the body panel and join the sleeve on the right side of the work using double crochet. Work from the front top edge down to the

underarm and back up to the top edge. The underarm point should meet the halfway point of the sleeve's depth.

F Repeat on the other side for the second sleeve.

G You now have a joined body and a sleeve that is attached on the underside but open along the top.

Top Front Sleeve/Shoulder Rows

Row 1:

Join in yarn at the outer sleeve point and work 1 row of granny stitch (see page 89) in the base colour, working inwards.

Rows 2–3:

Turn and continue following the instructions for granny stitch rows.

Row 4:

A Turn, chain 26.

B Miss 1 stitch.

C Slip stitch through the back bump of 25 chains to create a tie.

D Work a cluster into the next space, continue working clusters into each space along the row.

E Work 1 treble into third chain of the row below.

Row 5:

A Join in new colour with a slip stitch in space between treble and cluster at the wrist point.

B Work granny clusters along the row until you reach 4 cluster spaces before edge for sizes XS to 2XL and 5 cluster spaces before edge for sizes 3XL to 5XL.

C Work your final treble in the next space.

D Turn.

Row 6:

A Chain 3.

B Work the next cluster in the next space.

C Continue working 1 cluster in each space along the row.

D Finish the row by working 1 treble into the third chain from the row below.

E Fasten off.

Repeat on top front of the other side.

Top Back Rows

Row 1:

Join in at the outer sleeve point and work 1 row of granny stitch in the base colour, working inwards.

Rows 2–4:

Turn and continue following the instructions for granny stitch rows, fasten off.

Row 5:

A Join in new colour with a slip stitch in the space between treble and cluster at the wrist point.

B Work granny clusters along the whole row up to the opposite wrist.

Row 6/Side 1:

A Turn.

B Chain 3.

C Work the same number of clusters as worked in your final front row.

D Finish with a single treble in the next space.

E Fasten off.

Row 6/Side 2:

A Join the top row colour with a slip stitch in the third chain at the opposite wrist point.

B Chain 3.

C Work the same number of clusters as worked in your final front row.

D Finish with a single treble in the next space.

E Fasten off.

Shoulder Join

A Turn the garment wrong side out.

B Using the same colour as used for the last top row, join in with an open crochet join along the shoulder seam on the inside of the garment. Follow the instructions on page 80 to join the shoulder.

C Repeat for the second shoulder/sleeve.

D Fasten off and turn right side out.

ADD THE CUFFS AND COLLAR

Cuff Extension

A If required for size (see chart), add cuff extensions to the sleeve edges. Do this using the granny stitch rounds method in your contrast colours.

B On the first round, when you reach the shoulder/sleeve joining point, work 1 treble into the first corner before the join.

C Work 2 treble crochets together, working the first part of the stitch in the same place as the treble and the second over the join in the next corner.

D Work 1 more treble in the same place, this creates a cluster over the join.

E Continue and join with a slip stitch in the third chain at the beginning to complete the round.

F Continue working granny stitch rounds as needed for the size, working in your chosen colour order.

G Fasten off.

Collar

A Using your base colour and the double crochet join, join 4 pentagons on the wrong side of the work. Remember, we don't want this join to be a design detail.

B Once your collar is joined, attach it to the neckline of the coatigan. Use stitch markers to hold it in place.

C Using the colour of the last body row stripe and the double crochet joining method (see page 81), join on the wrong side of the collar but the right side of the coatigan, this will hide the seam in the fold.

D Work through each stitch, working 2 stitches over any chains/treble posts.

E Fasten off.

FINISHING

A Sew in any remaining yarn ends.

B Block if desired.

TOP TIPS

To work a classic collar, use your colour mix to work four rows of granny stitch. For the first row, work 1 cluster in each space and over each chain/treble post. You should have a total of 19 clusters for sizes XS to 2XL and 23 clusters for sizes 3XL–5XL. Continue for a total of four rows.

You can easily transform this design into a cropped jacket by omitting the bottom row of extended body squares. Instead, work a row of double crochet around the outer edge, adding a few more slip stitch ties at the front of the jacket.

SIZE	MEASUREMENTS		BODY EXTENDED SQUARES			SLEEVES THREE-ROUND SQUARES			APPROXIMATE METERAGE M (YD)		
	FLAT CHEST WIDTH CM (IN)	BODY LENGTH CM (IN)	SQUARE EXTENSION ROUNDS	TOTAL SQUARES	SIDE EDGE ROWS	THREE-ROUND MINI SQUARES PER SLEEVE (DEPTH X LENGTH)	TOTAL SQUARES	CUFF EXTENSION ROUNDS	TOTAL	BASE COLOUR JOIN, LOWER STIPE	CONTRAST COLOURS SQUARES COLLAR, UPPER STRIPE
XS	52 (20½)	64 (25¼)	7	8	–	2 x 3	12	5	1180 (1291)	285 (312)	895 (979)
S	60 (23½)	72 (28⅜)	8	8	–	2 x 3	12	5	1340 (1466)	295 (323)	1045 (1143)
M	66 (26in)	78 (30¾)	9	8	–	2 x 3	12	–	1440 (1575)	315 (345)	1125 (1230)
L	70 (27½)	82 (32¼)	10	8	–	2 x 3	12	–	1610 (1761)	330 (361)	1280 (1400)
XL	77 (30⅜)	82 (32¼)	10	8	2	2 x 3	12	–	1725 (1887)	345 (378)	1380 (1509)
2XL	81 (32)	82 (32¼)	10	8	3	2 x 3	12	–	1780 (1947)	350 (383)	1430 (1564)
3XL	86 (33⅞)	82 (32¼)	10	8	5	2 x 3	12	–	1915 (2095)	355 (389)	1560 (1706)
4XL	92 (36¼)	90 (35½)	11	8	4	3 x 2	12	5	2180 (2385)	340 (372)	1840 (2013)
5XL	95 (37½)	90 (35½)	11	8	5	3 x 2	12	5	2240 (2450)	345 (378)	1895 (2072)

Bonnet

The best bonnet for keeping your bonce warm! Bonnets are no longer just for babies, this Scandi-style bonnet uses the square and pentagon shapes to achieve that perfect, snug fit. You can even team it up with the Neckerchief Scarf to create a full hood design for ultimate winter protection!

TOP TIPS

If you want to give the bonnet a little bit more neck protection, then why not add a section of rib stitch to the bottom edge before adding the edging. If you are adding ribbing, work the edging in rows, back and forth across the front edge and add the ties to the bottom edge of the rib.

YARN WEIGHT
Aran (worsted)

HOOK SIZE
4.5mm/US size 7
(or to match tension)

TENSION
One single square motif = 10 x 10cm (4 x 4in)

SIZE
Flat width, from back of head to opening 25cm (10in). Full face opening length 25cm (10in)

SAMPLES
Two design variations are shown:

Variation 1: Hood/bonnet/scarf combination worked in 1 strand DK and 1 strand mohair to get aran weight. 2 colour design with outer round and join in same colour. Worked with double crochet join.
Variation 2: Bonnet worked in acrylic aran yarn with black base colour and 8 contrast colours joined with whip stitch.

APPROXIMATE METERAGE
Total for bonnet: 190m (208 yd)
Total for hood: 360m (394 yd)

TOTAL SHAPES
Bonnet: Ten squares and one pentagon

10 1

Hood : 14 Squares, 3 mini squares and 4 pentagons

14 3 4

BONNET

Step by Step Pattern Guide

SQUARES JOIN X 2

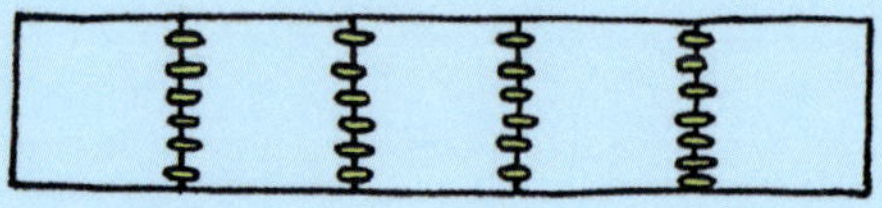

BONNET BODY

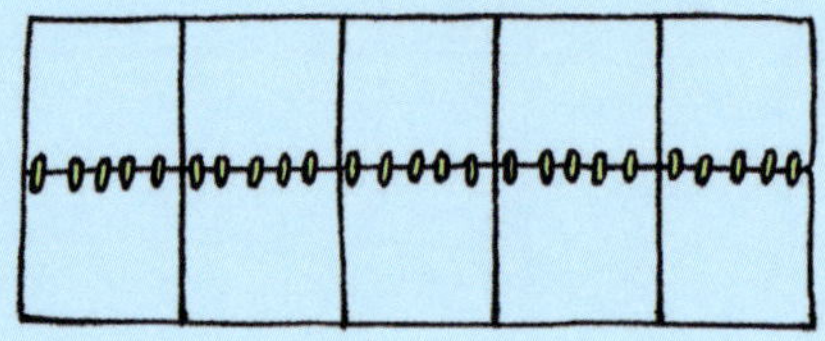

BONNET JOIN

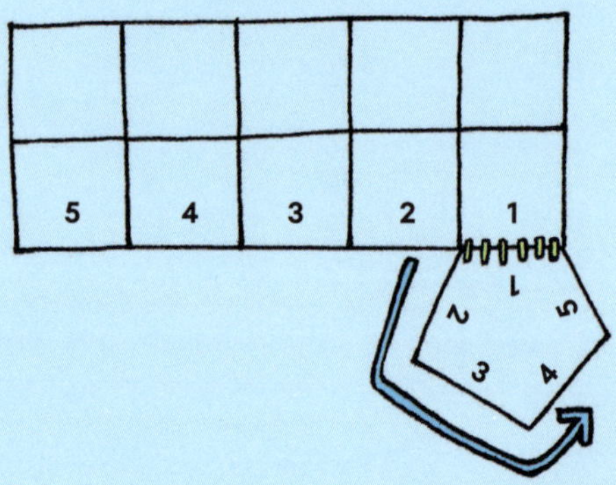

BONNET EDGING

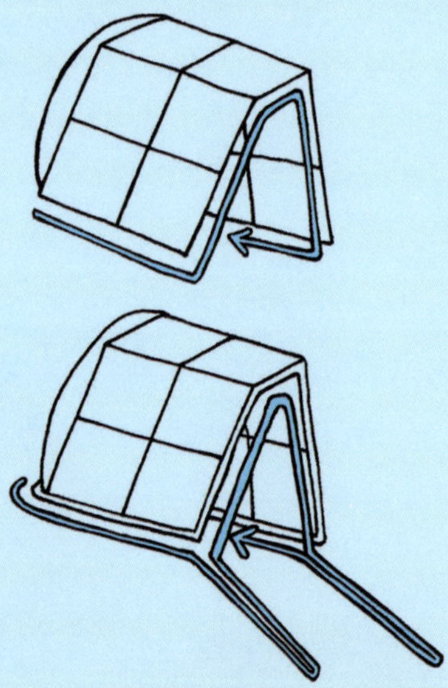

HOOD/BONNET COMBO

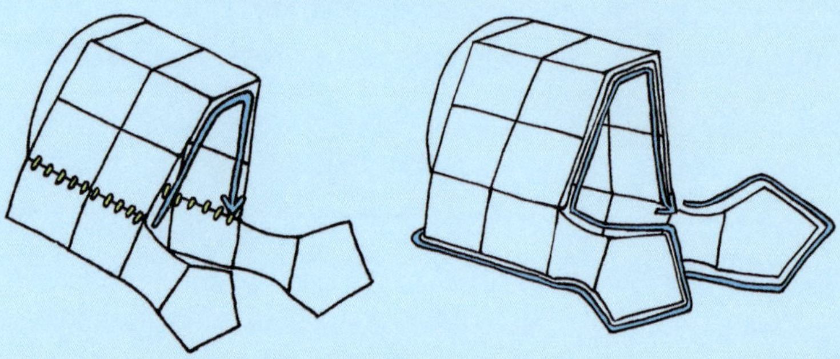

Getting Started

SHAPES

Make 10 squares and one pentagon. If you want to make the bonnet/hood combo then also add the shapes from the Neckerchief Scarf to this. This project works best with a solid join, so use the double crochet join (see page 81) or either of the sewn joins (see pages 78–79). Fasten off all full-sized shapes with the length of tail determined by the join you wish to use.

VARIATION 1 COLOURWAY

- Rounds 1–3: main colour
- Round 4: base colour

Instructions

JOINING

Squares Join/Bonnet Body Join

A Use your long tails to join your squares into two strips of five in your preferred closed-join method.

B With your base colour, join both strips together using the same joining method.

Bonnet Join

A Working in your base colour, and following the arrangement shown in the diagram, join the pentagon to the squares to close up the back of the bonnet. You can use stitch markers to hold the pieces together while you work.

B Your starting point for the join will become the centre back of your bonnet. If you are right-handed, join in an anticlockwise direction. If you are joining with a double crochet join, remember to work this on the inside of your bonnet.

BONNET EDGING

Round 1

A Using your base colour and starting with the yarn on your hook, join in at the centre back point of the bonnet, in the pentagon corner chain space, using a double crochet join.

B Work 1 round of double crochet around the whole outer edge of bonnet, working into each stitch (see page 86).

C Work (double crochet, chain 1, double crochet) into the front bonnet corner points.

D Join into the first double crochet with a slip stitch to complete the round.

Round 2

A Chain 1.

B Work 1 double crochet into each stitch until you reach the front corner.

C Chain 41 stitches.

D Miss 1 chain and double crochet into the back bump of the next 40 stitches to create a bonnet tie.

E Double crochet back into the corner chain to anchor.

F Double crochet into each stitch up to the next corner.

G Repeat steps C to E.

H Double crochet up to start of round.

I Join with a slip stitch in the first chain of the round.

J Fasten off.

FINISHING

A. Sew in any remaining ends.

B. Block the piece to finish.

HOOD COMBO JOIN

A If you are making the hood/bonnet combo, follow the bonnet pattern up to the bonnet edging.

B Follow the neckerchief scarf pattern up to the bow ends, working in the same tension as for the bonnet.

C Using your base colour, join the Neckerchief neck squares along the bottom edge of the bonnet, matching up the lines of the squares.

D If you are joining in crochet on the inside continue in the same yarn to the edge, if you are sewing your joins start in the same place with a slip stitch join.

E Turn to work on the right side (starting at the inner edge of face opening) chain 1, work a double crochet into each stitch along edge until you are opposite the small square.

F Follow the Neckerchief Scarf edging technique (see page 127), working slip stitches across the small squares and then switching back to double crochet for the other edges.

G Edge the outer scarf edge until you reach the starting chain.

H Work another row of double crochet across the face opening.

I Join into the stitch that meets the small square with a slip stitch.

J Fasten off.

TOP TIP

This is a great stash buster project, use up all your odds and ends of DK yarn to make lots of different stripes. You could even embrace patchwork-quilt style and use the half 'n' half square mixed with the granny square in the body of your jumper!

Patchwork Jumper

The Patchwork Jumper is made from a mixture of squares and hexis put together to create a graphic effect! With its relaxed shaping and oversized fit, it's the perfect choice for your new favourite jumper. You can make it with full-length sleeves, short sleeves or no sleeves at all for a fun sweater vest shape – the choice is yours! Because this piece is made up of lots of motifs, countless colour patterns can be created with its shapes – go graphic in monochrome, use a colour pop mix for summer or opt for tonal – what's the perfect combination for you?

YARN WEIGHT
DK (light worsted)

HOOK SIZE
4mm/US size G-6
(or to match tension)

TENSION
One single square motif = 10 x 10cm (4 x 4in)

SIZE
XS–5XL, see chart on page 161

EASE
30–40cm (11¾–15¾in) oversized fit

SAMPLE DESIGNS
Two design variations are shown:

Variation 1: Size S. Worked in an acrylic DK yarn. Long-sleeve jumper in a graphic two-colour pattern. Worked in black and white mixing the order of colour in the rounds/rows in each shape. Joined in black with black rib neckline. Shown on model sized S/M. Size down if you want a closer fit.

Variation 2: Size 4XL. Worked in a cotton mix DK yarn. Sleeveless jumper in multiple colours. Shapes are worked with a brown centre and brown is used for the joins. Elsewhere a colour mix of 10 other colours is used.

Variation 3: See page 6, version of variation 2 colourway with short sleeves in size 2XL.

APPROXIMATE METERAGE
Total meterage will be determined by your chosen size, see chart.

TOTAL SHAPES:
82–128, total will be determined by your chosen size, see chart

PATCHWORK JUMPER

Step by Step Pattern Guide

CONTRAST JOIN, PIN CORNERS TOGETHER AND JOIN SHORT ROWS

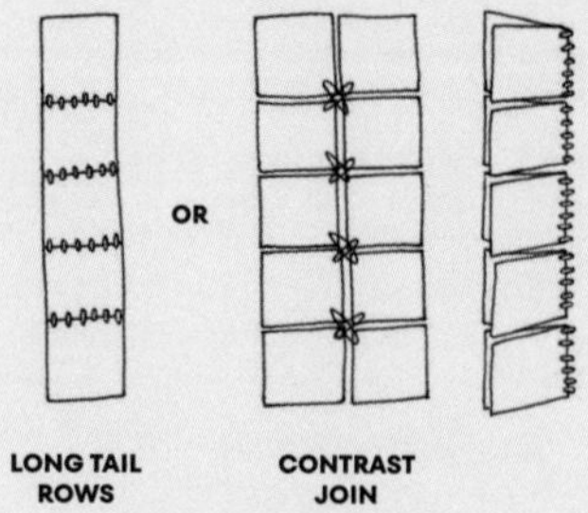

WORK ALONG JOINING MORE BODY ROWS

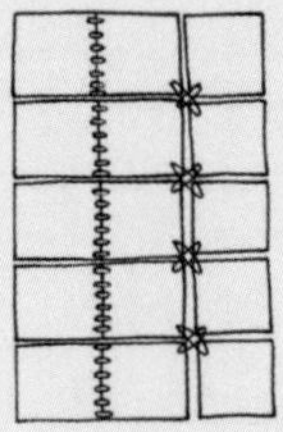

JOIN ALONG LONG STRIPS

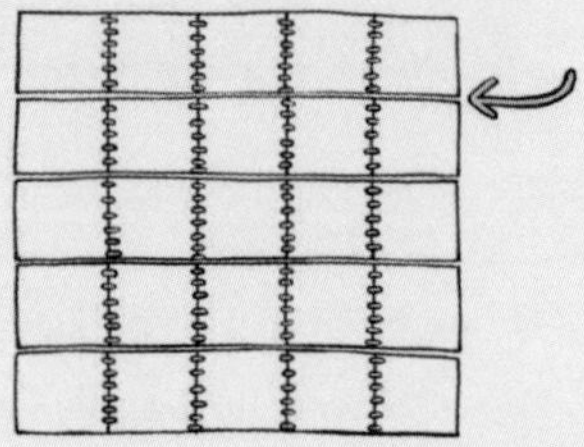

WORK BODY PANELS X 2. ADD BODY SIZING ROWS (1) AND ADD SHOULDER SHAPING (2)

WORK JUMPER SHOULDER JOINS

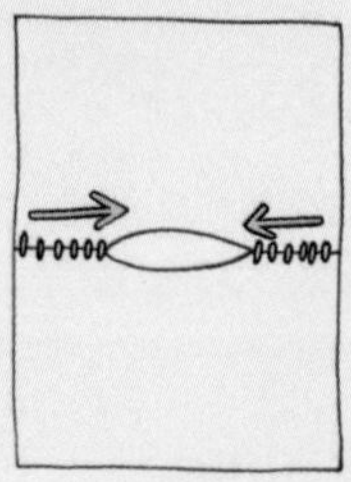

SLEEVE SIZES IN CM(IN):

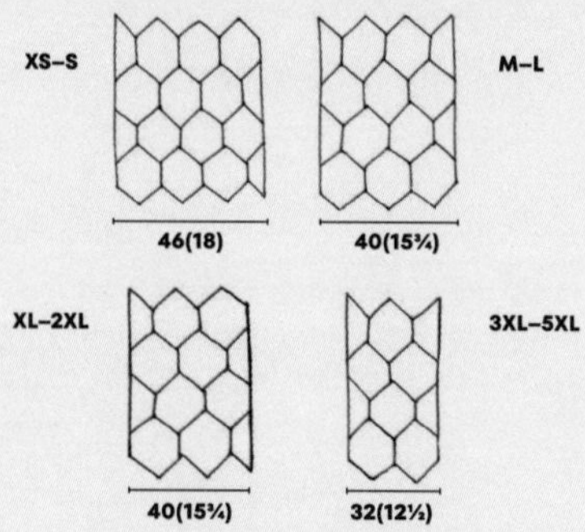

JOIN SLEEVE ROWS

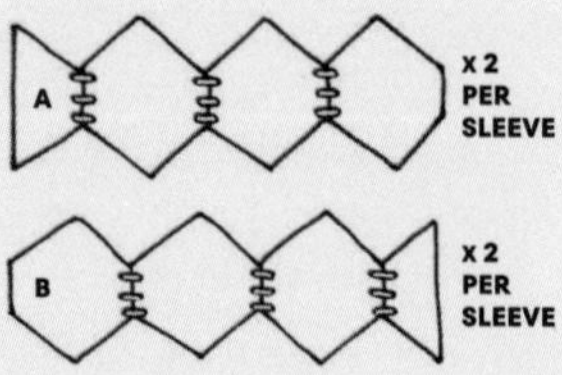

JOIN UP ROWS TO COMPLETE SLEEVE TUBE

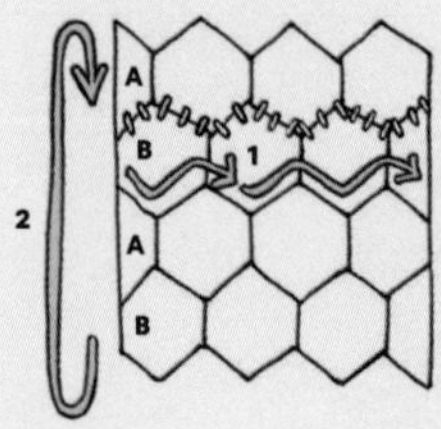

JOIN SLEEVE TO BODY

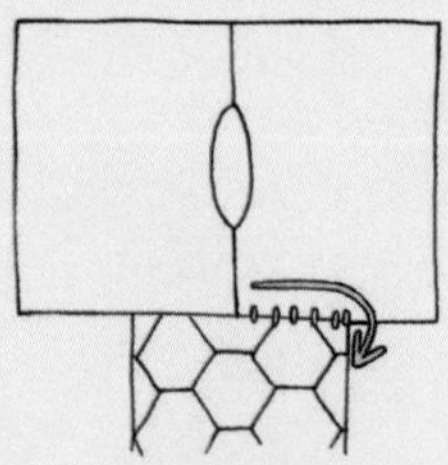

JOIN REST OF SIDE (1), ADD BOTTOM EDGING (2), ADD SLEEVE EDGE (3)

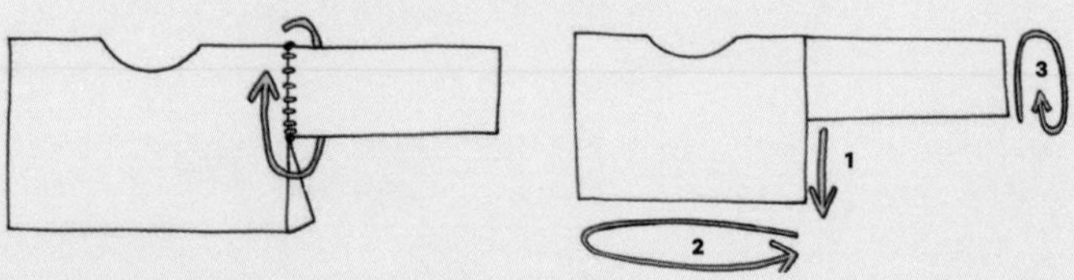

COMPLETE WITH NECK RIB

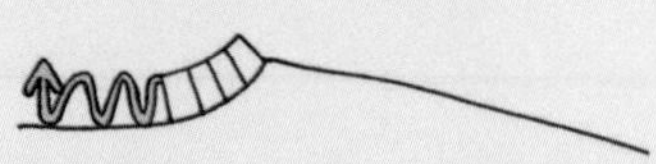

Getting Started

SHAPES

Follow the chart to make the correct number of squares, hexagons and half hexis for your jumper size. This design has contrasting sleeves and body; the sleeves are worked in hexagons and half hexis and the body is made up of squares. The open crochet join (see page 80) is used for this garment. Use stitch markers to hold your pieces together as you join and work along longer edges in one go. The sizing of this piece is adjusted by changing the number of squares and sizing rounds for the body. For the sleeve width, the number of shapes is increased by one round/row for the larger sizes and the number of shapes in the length of the sleeve is adjusted too. Use the chart and diagrams to check you are making the correct size garment. Now, it might seem odd that the smallest size garment has the longest length sleeve, but this is because our design is a boxy drop-sleeve in shape. We also have to take into account the width of our jumper body for our sleeve length, so when these sleeves are teamed with the body piece, they will be the perfect size.

COLOURWAY

This design is shown in two colour variations: high contrast black and white and a rich colour pop mix. For the black and white variation, the bold patterning is achieved by mixing the colour order in the shapes in eight different ways, creating strong patterns by playing with different round colour sequences. If you want to make this design, divide your total number of shapes by eight and plan your eight variations or use the table below to help you distribute the two colours as evenly as possible. Make the number of shapes needed for each colour batch. It's important to lay out your shapes before joining to check the pattern distribution.

ROUND/ ROW	COLOUR ORDER							
1	A	B	A	B	A	B	A	B
2	B	A	A	B	A	B	A	B
3	A	B	B	A	B	A	A	B
4	B	A	B	A	A	B	B	A
5 (for sleeves sizes L-5XL)	A	B	B	A	A	B	B	A

Instructions

BODY PANELS

A Lay out the body squares in two panels to make sure the colours and square patterns are distributed evenly.
B Working in the joining colour, join the squares together into two panels using the open crochet joining technique (see page 80).
C Join the short edges first and then join the longer rows. If you are using long tails to join, or a contrast join, use stitch markers or small safety pins to hold the corners of the squares together while you join them. Pin the squares as you work, rather than pinning the whole piece at once.
D Join the shorter rows for the depth of the jumper first.
E Then join the longer rows for the width of the jumper.
F Fasten off and sew in yarn ends.

BODY SIZING ROWS

Refer to the chart on page 161to see if you need to add body sizing rows along the edges of the front and back panels. If you do, work on the outside edge in a U-shape (not working the top edge).

A Join in at the top outside edge corner chain space and, using the chosen colour, work the additional rows in granny stitch rows. If you are working more than 1 row, change the colour with each new row.
B Follow the granny stitch rows pattern on page 89. In the bottom corner chain spaces work (cluster, chain 2, cluster).
C Repeat granny stitch rows to required size, see chart for reference.
D Fasten off.
E Repeat on the second panel.

SHOULDER SHAPING

Repeat for each body panel.

A Mark the desired width of your head hole with stitch markers and remember to allow a bit more space if you're adding a rib finish. For reference, the small sample neck width is 22cm (8¾in) and the 4XL is 30cm (11¾in).
B Count the stitches from the marked neck edge to the outer edge of the sweater.
C Divide this number in half. The half closest to the neck opening will be worked in treble stitches.
D Divide the remaining half by three and split the stitches evenly between slip stitches, double crochets, and half trebles.

E Using your chosen yarn colour, work the shoulder shaping from the outside edge, work in the order of smallest stitch to tallest, working slip stitches first, then double crochet, half trebles and finishing at the treble stitches closest to the neck. If you are working over extension rows, work two stitches over each treble post.

SLEEVES

Join the hexagons and half hexis into two tubes using the open crochet joining method.

A Work the number of hexagons and half hexis needed for your size. Please note, sizes L–5XL also use 5-round/row hexagons for sizing adjustments.
B Lay the sleeve panels out to arrange the colour design.
C Following the diagram, join the short edges into rows using either the yarn from the long-tail fasten off or new yarn.
D Using new yarn, join the longer rows together along the zigzag edge to make a flat panel.
E Join the top and bottom edges to make a cylinder and complete the sleeve.
F Repeat for the second sleeve.

SHOULDER JOIN

A Working in your chosen colour, join the top edges of the front and back panels together to create the shoulder seam. Place right sides together and, working on the inside, join using the double crochet joining technique (see page 81). Repeat on both shoulders.

JUMPER JOINING

A Attach the sleeves to the body panels. Place right sides together and, with the body panel opened out, use stitch markers to line up the centre of the sleeve (centre of half hexi) with the top shoulder seam. Working on the inside (wrong side) of the garment, join using the open crochet joining technique (see page 80). Start at the top shoulder join and work down.
B Line up the clusters as well as you can, the aim is to evenly join these in. Where the side of a hexi meets the top edge of a square or granny stitch row, the sides of the rows are equal to one cluster group.
C When you have worked down the edge to reach the centre of the half hexi at the underarm point, you will need to fold the body panel along the shoulder and work back up the other side. To make sure this lines up, check that you have the same number of clusters from the jumper bottom edge to the underarm point on both sides.
D Work back into the centre point of the half hexi and into corresponding space on the second body panel.
E Work along the edge back to the shoulder point, fasten off.
F Repeat for the other sleeve.
G To join the remaining body side seams (1), use your joining colour and the open crochet joining technique, work from the bottom edge of the jumper to the underarm point.
H Fasten off.
I Repeat steps H and I for the other side.
J Sew in all yarn ends.

BOTTOM AND CUFF EDGING

A For the bottom edging (2), join in with your chosen colour at the side seam and work the number of extra rounds as given in the chart in granny stitch rows.
B Join with a slip stitch into the third chain at the beginning of the last round to complete.
C Fasten off.
D Join in with your chosen colour at the cuff underarm point (3), work 2 rounds of double crochet (see page 86) working 2 stitches over the side of each treble in the first round.
E Fasten off and sew in yarn ends.

NECK RIB

Work a 6-double-crochet-wide rib in the main/joining colour.

A Using your chosen colour, join in at the inner neck shoulder seam with a double crochet join.
B Chain 6 + 1 turning chain.
C Work rib pattern around the neck edge (see page 91). Work two rows of rib pattern over the side of treble posts around the neck.
D At the last stitch, join the rib by working the first and last rows together with a double crochet join on the inside of garment.
E Fasten off and sew in yarn ends.

FINISHING

Block if desired, following the instructions on page 93.

TOP TIP

For a sleeveless piece, you can adapt the jumper for a very different look. For this variation, miss the sleeves out and finish by making the armhole the depth of your choosing – I recommend a nice deep armhole to get those larger, flowy summer sleeves through. Work one round of granny stitch around the armhole edge to finish off. If you want the T-shirt look, halve the number of shapes in the length of your sleeve.

SIZE	MEASUREMENTS			BODY X 2			SLEEVES X 2	TOTAL SHAPES			APPROXIMATE METERAGE (YD)		
	CHEST FLAT WIDTH IN CM (IN)	BODY LENGTH IN CM (IN)	SLEEVE LENGTH X DEPTH IN CM (IN)	SQUARES WIDTH X DEPTH	SIZING ROWS	BOTTOM EDGE ROUNDS	HEXAGON/ HALF HEXI EXTRA ROUNDS/ ROWS	BODY SQUARES	SLEEVE HEXAGONS/ HALF HEXI	ALL	TOTAL	BODY SQUARES, SIZING ROWS, JOINING, NECK	SLEEVES HEXAGONS/HALF HEXIS, JOINING
XS	50 (19¾)	52 (20½)	46 x 22 (18 x 8½)	5 x 5	–	1	–	50	24/8	82	1645 (1799)	935 (1023)	710 (776)
S	56 (22)	55 (21¾)	46 x 22 (18 x 8½)	5 x 5	+3	1	–	50	24/8	82	1730 (1892)	1020 (1115)	710 (777)
M	62 (24½)	53 (20⅞)	40 x 22 (15¾ x 8½)	6 x 5	+1	1	–	60	20/8	88	1715 (1876)	1110 (1214)	605 (662)
L	70 (27½)	53 (20⅞)	40 x 22 (15¾ x 8½)	7 x 5	–	2	–	70	20/8	98	1835 (2007)	1230 (1345)	605 (662)
XL	76 (30)	55 (21¾)	40 x 22 (15¾ x 8½)	7 x 5	+3	1	+1	70	16/8	94	2065 (2259)	1390 (1520)	675 (739)
2XL	82 (32¼)	63 (24¾)	40 x 27 (15¾ x 10½)	8 x 6	+1	1	+1	96	16/8	120	2340 (2560)	1665 (1821)	675 (739)
3XL	86 (33¾)	65 (25½)	32 x 27 (12½ x 10½)	8 x 6	+3	1	+1	96	12/8	116	2330 (2549)	1790 (1958)	540 (591)
4XL	90 (35½)	65 (25½)	32 x 27 (12½ x 10½)	9 x 6	–	3	+1	108	12/8	128	2405 (2630)	1865 (2040)	540 (591)
5XL	96 (37¾)	65 (25½)	32 x 27 (12½ x 10½)	9 x 6	+3	1	+1	108	12/8	128	2610 (2855)	2070 (2264)	540 (591)

Tabard

This tie-up tabard is a great throw-on top, perfect for wearing over dresses or blouses with big billowy sleeves due to its low side ties – the perfect additional layer for a spring or summer outfit! Go graphic, use block colour or opt for classic striped granny squares for very different looks; you can really play around with this simply shaped garment.

TOP TIPS

Work in a thinner cotton DK with loose tension to match original tension size to create a lacy weight summer version, perfect to wear as a beach cover up.

This top style also works well for growing kids or maternity wear as the ties allow for a range of sizes. If you are making a kids' version, size down your yarn or reduce your square rounds to make it smaller.

YARN WEIGHT
Aran (worsted)

HOOK SIZE
5.5mm/US size I-9
(or to match tension)

TENSION
One four-round square = 11.5 x 11.5cm (4½ x 4½ in)

SIZE
XS–5XL, see chart on page 166

EASE
Varying ease due to ties – between tight fitting and loose fit.

SAMPLE
Size M/L. Worked in merino Aran yarn. Graphic two-colour pattern using half 'n' half squares. Joined with mattress stitch. Contrast two-colour rib neckline. Sample size M/L, shown on size M and size XL to show fit options.

APPROXIMATE METERAGE
Total meterage will be determined by your chosen size, see chart.

TOTAL SHAPES
18 to 24 squares and 4 half squares, depending on size, see chart.

18 4

TABARD

Step by Step Pattern Guide

LAYOUT AND PIN TWO BODY PANELS

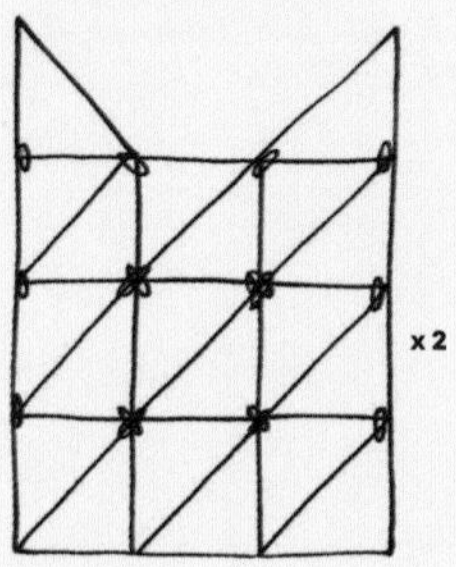

ATTACHED TOGETHER, JOIN FOLLOWING ORDER 1–4

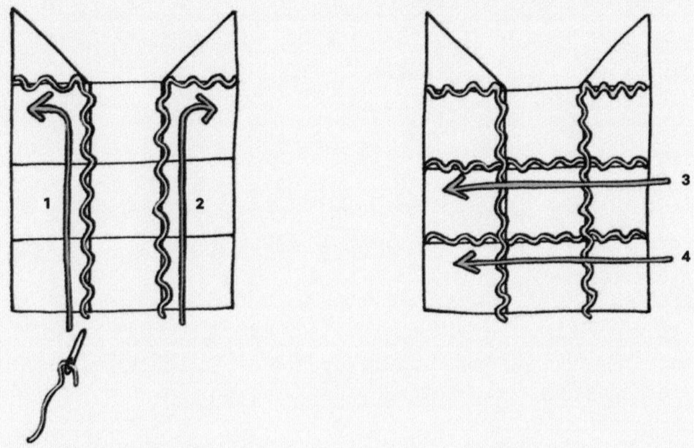

JOIN SHOULDER POINT (1) AND ADD OUTSIDE BORDER ROUNDS (2)

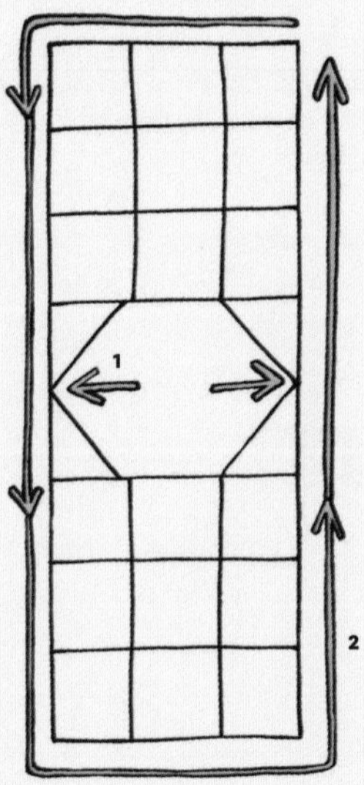

ADD SIDE TIES AND LOWER SHAPING

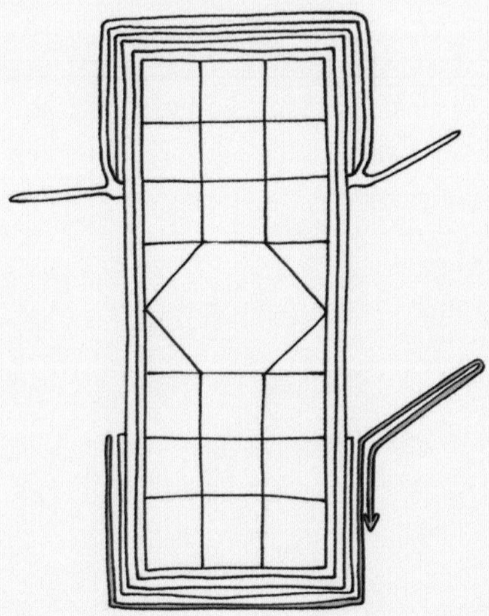

ADD NECK RIBBING

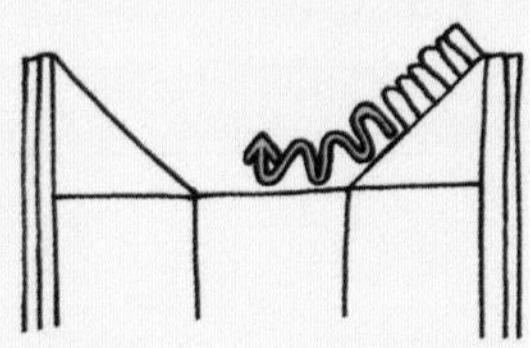

Getting Started

SHAPES

Make 18 to 24 full squares (depending on size). You could choose to make granny squares or follow the sample design by using the half 'n' half square and make four half squares for the neck shaping by just working side 1 of the half 'n' half square. The sample is joined in mattress stitch for an invisible join but all join types will work for this make. Fasten off squares and join with new yarn unless long-tail joining works for your individual customization of the design. Keep long tails on half squares.

COLOURWAY

To follow the graphic two-colour sample, work your squares in a two-colour design and make two half squares in each of your colours. When constructing your tabard, use half on the back and half on the front. If you are following the sample this will make a front and back that aren't the same, and the colours will be inverted on the other side to evenly use up your yarns. Neck rib is also worked in two colours for a striped effect.

Instructions

JOINING

Body Join

A Lay out the squares and half squares to make up your body panels.
B Make sure the half squares on one panel have long tails on their top shoulder points.
C Use stitch markers to hold the design in place.
D Join in with a new yarn and work mattress stitch (see page 79, or your chosen joining method).
E Following the diagram, first join up the body and across the half square at the neck (1).
F Repeat for the next row (2).
G Join across the width of the panel (2, 3).
H Repeat for the other body panel.

Shoulder Join

A Once your body panels are joined, use the half square tails at the top shoulder points to join along the last treble/fake treble of the final rounds of each side.
B Using mattress stitch or whip stitch (see page 78), join the half square points to create your shoulder join and close your neckline.

OUTER ROUNDS

A Follow the sizing chart to work the number of outer rounds you need for your size.
B Depending on how many outer rounds and tie rounds you need, divide your colours evenly between them if you are working in stripes.
C Start in any corner and follow the granny stitch round instructions (page 88).
D On your first round, when you reach the shoulder join point, work 1 treble into the space between the last treble of corner 1 of the first half square.
E Work 2 trebles together, working the first part of the stitch in the same place as the first treble and the second over the join in between the treble of the corner of your second half square.
F Work 1 more treble into the same place, this creates a cluster over the shoulder join.
G Continue with the round and repeat steps D to F on the other shoulder.
H At the end of the round, join with a slip stitch in the third chain.
I Continue working the number of granny rounds needed for the size in your chosen colour order.
J Fasten off.

TIES AND LOWER SHAPING

Row 1:

A Counting from the bottom corner, including the corner space, place a stitch marker 10 (10, 12, 12) cluster gaps up along the side of each body panel.
B Using your chosen yarn colour, join in with in a slip stitch at the space with the marker.
C Chain 3. Working into next space, follow the granny stitch rows instructions.
D Work around the lower edge of the panels. In the corners work (cluster, chain 2, cluster).
E Continue up to the stitch marker space on the opposite side.
F Work 1 treble in the marked space.

Rows 2–3 (for sizes 3XL–5XL only):

G Repeat steps C to F (replacing stitch marker space with last space) for 2 more rows.

Rows 2/4:

H On final shaping row, chain 54. (This counts as 50 chain cord, 1 turning chain and 3 chains that work as a fake treble)
I Miss 1 stitch.
J Work double crochet into the back bump of the chain for 50 stitches to create the tie.
K Work a cluster into the next space.
L Continue, following the granny stitch cluster row instructions until you reach the last space between clusters.

M When just the space between chain and cluster remains, chain 51 stitches.
N Miss 1 stitch.
O Work double crochet into the back bump of the chain for 50 stitches to create the tie.
P Chain 3.
Q Work a slip stitch into the third chain from row below to join.
R Fasten off.

NECK RIB

Worked in stripes in two colours – colour A and colour B.

A Join in colour A with a slip stitch over the chain at shoulder point.
B Chain 7.
C Miss 1 stitch.
D Double crochet 6 stitches along the chain.
E Follow rib instructions on page 91.
F If you are working a 2-colour stripe rib, work colour A to first anchor double crochet stitch, change to colour B for the second. Work row and return row in colour B and then switch colours after the first anchor stitch.
G Close the stitch working the final part of the double crochet in colour B.
H Leave colour A at the back of the work and double crochet over next chain with colour B.
I Turn.
J Miss 2 stitches.
K Work double crochet through the back loop for 6 stitches.
L Chain 1, turn.
M Double crochet through the back loop for 6 stitches.
N Anchor to neck with a double crochet over chain, work only the first half of double crochet in colour B.
O Pick up colour A and close the double crochet.
P Now leave colour B at the back of the work and continue with colour A.
Q Continue following this technique to work the colour stripe rib.
R For spacing, work 2 anchor stitches over the chain/ treble post sides of the of the half 'n' half squares and in each stitch along the square edges.
S At the last stitch, join the rib by working the first and last rows together with a double crochet join on the inside of the garment.
T Fasten off and sew in yarn ends.

FINISHING

A Sew in any remaining yarn ends.
B Block.

SIZE	MEASUREMENTS		BODY SQUARES X 2			BODY ROUNDS		TOTAL TWO BODY PANELS		APPROXIMATE METERAGE IN M (YDS)
	CHEST FLAT WIDTH IN CM (IN)	BODY LENGTH IN CM (IN)	SQUARES WIDTH X DEPTH	HALF SQUARES	EXTRA ROUNDS	OUTER ROUNDS	TIE ROWS	SQUARES	HALF SQUARES	TOTAL
XS–S	44 (17¼)	51 (20)	3 x 3	2	–	2	2	18	4	575 (629)
M–L	50 (19¾)	54 (21¼)	3 x 3	2	–	4	2	18	4	660 (722)
XL–2XL	60 (23½)	64 (25¼)	3 x 3	2	+1	4	2	18	4	840 (919)
3XL–5XL	71 (28)	64 (25¼)	4 x 3	2	+1	2	4	24	4	980 (1072)

Vest

With its oversized fit, deep neckline and zigzag bottom edge, this design is a fun take on the grandad-style sweater vest and is the perfect extra layer for all year round. This project makes use of three crochet shapes, the square, pentagon and hexagon and it's easy to customize; you could use a variation of the same pattern to create a cropped, more fitted, tie-front waistcoat, which also uses the half hexi!

YARN WEIGHT
Aran (light worsted)

HOOK SIZE
Vest: 5.5mm/US size I-9
(or to match tension)
Waistcoat: 4.5mm/US size 7
(or to match tension)

TENSION
Vest – one four-round square = 11.5 x 11.5cm (4½ x 4½in)
Waistcoat – one four-round square = 10 x 10cm (4 x 4in)

SIZE
XS–5XL, see chart on page 173

EASE
Vest: 17–32cm (6¾–12½in) oversized fit
Waistcoat: No ease, form fitting

SAMPLES
Two design variations are shown:

Vest: Size M/L is in alpaca/merino for the base colour and merino Aran yarn for the 10 contrast colours. Shapes are joined with double crochet in the base colour and the garment is finished with arm and neck ribbing. Sample shown on size S/M.

Waistcoat: Size XL/2XL worked in one strand of fine merino and one strand of mohair held together to make a 2ply mix. The mohair is brushed to finish. Joined with contrast double crochet join. Sample shown on size XL.

APPROXIMATE METERAGE
Total meterage will be determined by your chosen size, see chart

TOTAL SHAPES
23–34, total will be determined by your chosen size, see chart

VEST/WAISTCOAT

Step by Step Pattern Guide

JOIN
SIZES XS/S–M/L

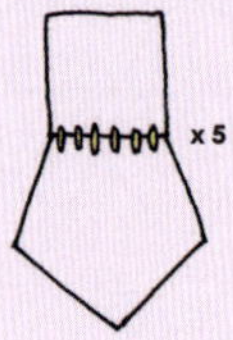

JOIN
SIZES XL/2XL–4XL/5XL

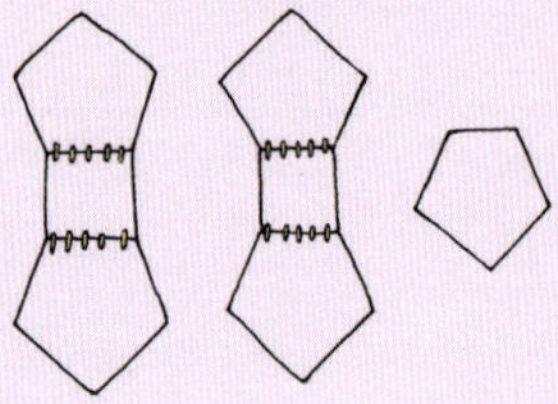

UPPER BACK JOIN
SIZES XS/S–M/L

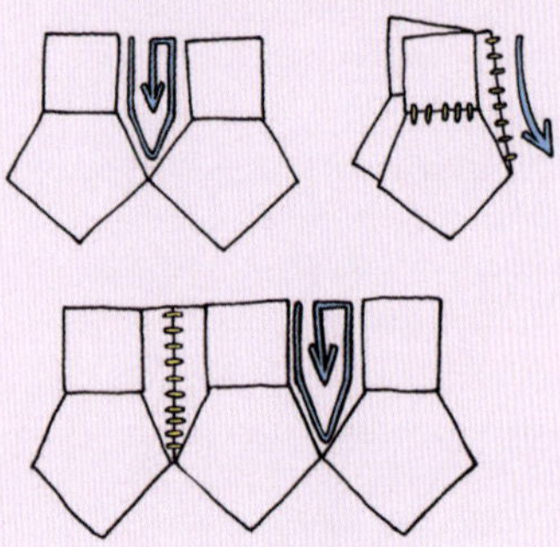

UPPER BACK JOIN
SIZES XL/2XL–3XL–5XL

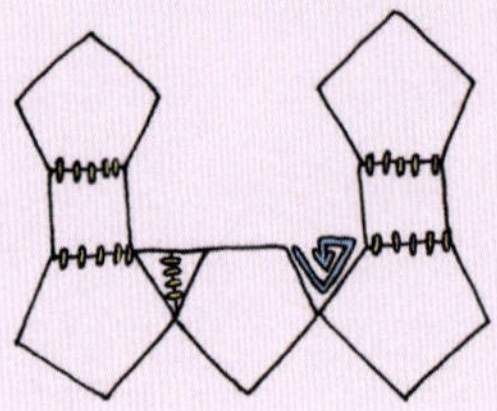

SHOULDER JOIN
SIZES XS/S–M/L

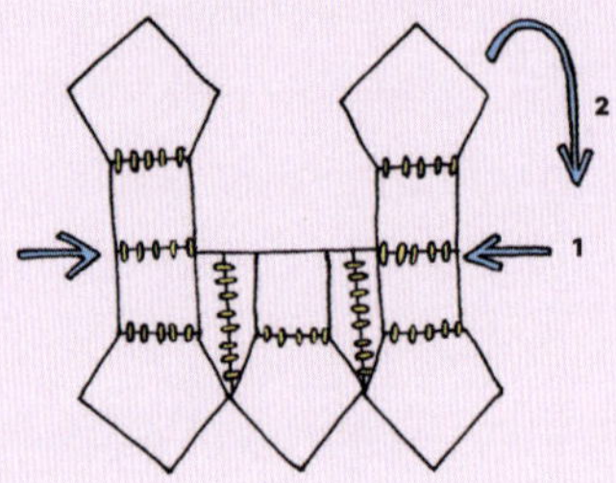

BODY JOIN

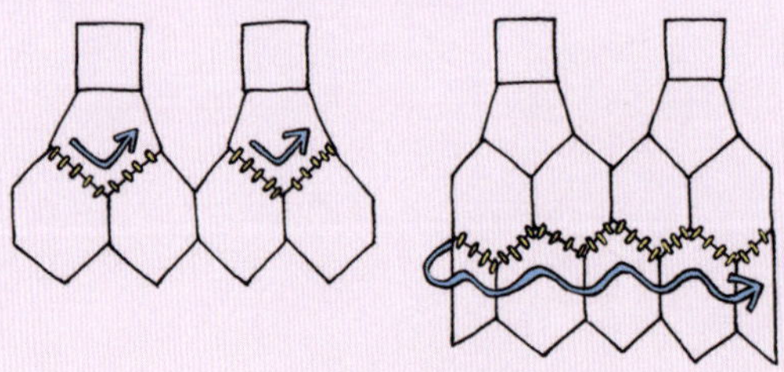

HEXAGON JOINS

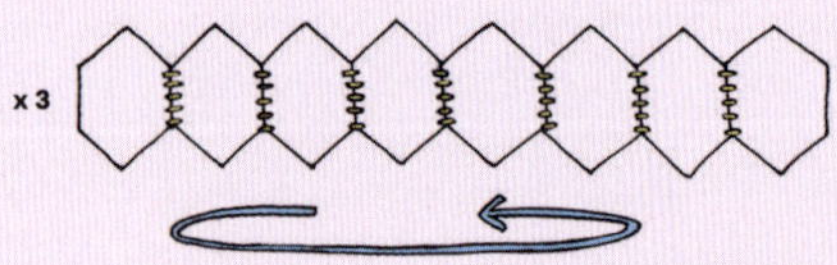

EDGING

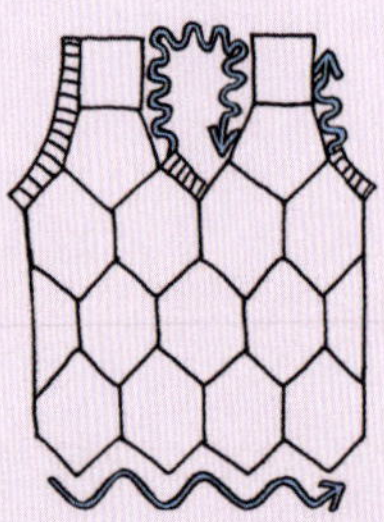

WAISTCOAT EDGING

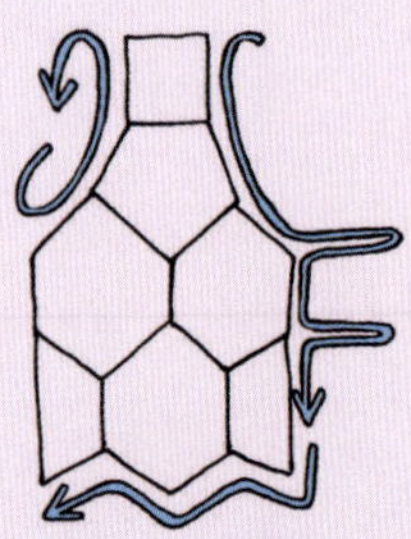

Getting Started

SHAPES

Make the number of shapes required for the size you are making as given in the chart onpage 173. Sizing for this pattern is adjusted by changing the number of shapes used, but for the larger sizes the shapes also have extension rounds. Fasten off shapes and join with contrast double crochet join.

COLOURWAY

Order for four-round shapes:

- Round 1: base colour (use travel-up colour technique, see page 73)
- Round 2: contrast colour
- Round 3: base colour
- Round 4: contrast colour

If you are making five- or six-round shapes, work the two colours in alternating order, making sure the outer round is in your contrast colour.

Instructions

JOINING

Square/Pentagon join

A Using your base colour, follow the diagram to join the squares and pentagons together in the correct formation for the size you are making.
B Work on the wrong side of the work and join with a double crochet join (see page 81, or your preferred joining method).

Back Shaping for Sizes XS–S and M–L

A Different stitch heights are used to create the infill to make the back shapes tessellate.
B Using your base colour, join in with a slip stitch in square corner space.
C Chain 3.

D Treble into each stitch along the side of your square.
E Treble into each stitch along the first side of your pentagon until 3 clusters remain.
F Half treble 3.
G Double crochet 3.
H To attach the next pentagon, join in with a double crochet in the first stitch of the second cluster up from the side corner.
I Double crochet 2.
J Half treble 3.
K Treble up to end of row/side of shapes. This completes your shaped infill.
L Fold shapes right sides together.
M Join with double crochet along the edge, working through each stitch.
N Continue past the last shaping double crochet and join the final clusters of each pentagon together up to the corner chain space.
O Fasten off.
P Repeat steps B to O to join the final back panel.

Back shaping for sizes XL–2XL and 3XL–5XL

A Different stitch heights are used to create the infill to make the back shapes tessellate.
B Using your base colour, join in with a slip stitch on the front of the work at square and pentagon join stitch.
C Chain 4.
D Double treble into each stitch along the first side of your pentagon until 4 clusters remain.
E Treble 3.
F Half treble 3.
G Double crochet 3.
H To attach the next pentagon, join in with a double crochet in the first stitch of the second cluster up from the side corner.
I Double crochet 2.
J Half treble 3.
K Treble 3.
L Double treble up to pentagon corner space. This completes your shaped infill.
M Fold shapes right sides together.
N Join with double crochet along the edge, working through each stitch.
O Continue past last shaping double crochet and join the final clusters of each pentagon together up to the corner chain space.
P Fasten off.
Q Repeat steps B to P to join final back panel.

Shoulder Join

A For sizes XS/S and M/L, join squares along the shoulders on the wrong side of the work using double crochet.

B For sizes XL/2XL and 3XL–5XL, fold along centre line of the square to get your shoulder line.

Hexagon Joins

A Using your base colour, join the edges of your hexagons together in a row. For size XS, join 7 hexagons per row, for all other sizes join 8.

B Join the edges with a double crochet join on the wrong side of the work.

C Join first and last hexagon of row together to form a ring.

D Repeat steps A to C until you have 3 hexagon rings. If you are making the waistcoat, make 1 strip of 7 and 1 strip of 6 hexagons with a half hexagon on either end. Leave as strips, do not join.

Top Front Body Join

Use stitch markers to hold the first hexagon ring in place beneath the top front and back panels.

A Using your base colour and working on the wrong side, double crochet join your top panel to your first hexagon ring.

B The first join attaches the top front and back panels and creates the armholes and neckline.

C You can use stitch markers to hold the hexagons in place by matching the corner points. Follow the diagram on page 170 for shaping. For size XS, with 7 hexagons, make the first round of hexagons match up at centre front and have fold at underarm.

D Using the double crochet joining method (see page 81), start on the front hexagon top point chain space which meets the side pentagon corner at the front.

E Work your join over the tail of the yarn you have added or any other ends that need to be hidden. This saves you from sewing them in at the end.

F Double crochet through both layers up to the next hexagon corner chain space.

G In the corner, work one double crochet through the hexagon corner and the pentagon point chain space that you have worked across.

H Work into the next hexagon corner chain space and then back into the same pentagon point chain space, joining with a double crochet.

I Work double crochet along the edge until you reach the next hexagon point chain space.

J Fasten off.

K Repeat steps D to J on the opposite side of front.

Top Back Body Join

A Using the double crochet joining method, start in the hexagon point chain space and join with a double crochet into the pentagon corner.

B Work your join over the tail of the yarn you have added or any other ends that need to be hidden. This saves you from sewing them in at the end.

C Double crochet through both layers up to next hexagon corner chain space.

D In corner, work one double crochet through hexagon corner and the pentagon point chain space that you have worked across.

E Work into the next hexagon corner chain space and then back into the same pentagon point chain space, joining with a double crochet.

F Work double crochet join along the edge until you reach the next hexagon point chain space.

G Double crochet through the hexagon point chain space and into the pentagon corner chain space.

H Double crochet through the same hexagon point chain space and into the next pentagon corner chain space.

I Repeat steps E to J until you have worked all the way across the back.

J Fasten off.

Body Join

A Use stitch markers to pin the next 2 rings of hexagons into place on the body.

B Following the same method as for the top back join, join the 2 rings of hexagons. If you are making the waistcoat, work from centre front around to opposite centre front.

NECKLINE AND ARMHOLES

Arm Ribbing

A Using the base colour and in the right side of the work, join in at the underarm point.

B Following the rib instructions (see page 91), work a 5-stitch rib around the armhole.

C Join the rib by working the first and last rows together with a double crochet join on the wrong side of the garment.

D Repeat on the opposite armhole.

Neck Ribbing

E Join in the base colour 6 stitches up on the right (left if left-handed) from the centre join.

F Double crochet 6 stitches to centre join, working your last stitch in the corner chain space.

G Work your next double crochet into the next corner chain space over the join.

H Work 1 double crochet into next stitch.

I Turn.

J Miss 2 stitches.

K Double crochet into the back loop of your first 6 double crochets.

L You have now set up your next rib, follow rib instructions and work around the neckline up to the last stitch.

M Once you have finished your final row, join the rib by working the last row and the edge of the first 6 rows together with a double crochet join on the inside of the garment.

N Fasten off.

EDGING AND FINISHING

Vest Variation

A Using the base colour, work 1 round of double crochet along the bottom edge. Follow the double crochet round instructions (see page 86).

B Sew in any remaining yarn ends.

C Block.

Waistcoat Variation

A Using a contrast colour, work 1 round of double crochet along the armhole edges.

B Work 1 round of double crochet along the outer edge adding 25-stitch slip stitch cords at the front hexagon corner points. See cord technique on the Colour Lovin' Coatigan (page 147)

C Sew in any remaining yarn ends.

D Block.

TOP TIPS

If you want a less oversized look for your vest, size down. If you are already working the smallest size, match your tension to the waistcoat tension. If you want a roomier waistcoat, size up and match the vest tension. Remember, customizing the fit will affect your yarn usage and meterage.

If you want the back shaping to blend in rather than be a feature, use the yarn colour that matches the shapes you're working into for the stitches across. If you are changing colour mid-row to match each shape, change your yarn colour at the last stage of the stitch before the stitch that needs to be a different colour.

VEST									
SIZE	MEASUREMENTS		BODY SHAPES				APPROXIMATE METERAGE IN M (YDS)		
	CHEST FLAT WIDTH IN CM (IN)	BODY LENGTH IN CM (IN)	SQUARES	HEXAGONS	PENTAGONS	EXTRA ROUNDS	TOTAL	BASE COLOUR JOIN, RIB	CONTRAST COLOURS
XS–S	46 (18⅛)	64 (25¼)	5	21	5	–	955 (1045)	560 (613)	395 (432)
M–L	60 (23½)	64 (25¼)	5	24	5	–	1085 (1187)	645 (706)	440 (481)
XL–2XL	72 (28⅜)	73 (28¾)	2	24	5	+1	1360 (1488)	705 (771)	655 (717)
3XL–5XL	84 (33)	86 (33⅞)	2	24	5	+2	1755 (1920)	995 (1089)	760 (831)

WAISTCOAT								
SIZE	MEASUREMENTS		BODY SHAPES					APPROXIMATE METERAGE IN M (YDS)
	CHEST FLAT WIDTH IN CM (IN)	BODY LENGTH IN CM (IN)	SQUARES	HEXAGONS	PENTAGONS	HALF HEXI	EXTRA ROUNDS	TOTAL
XS–S	41 (16⅛)	49 (19¼)	5	13	5	2	–	520 (569)
M–L	54 (21¼)	49 (19¼)	5	15	5	2	–	575 (629)
XL–2XL	64 (25¼)	54 (21¼)	2	15	5	2	+1	740 (810)
3XL–5XL	74 (29⅛)	61 (24)	2	15	5	2	+2	1005 (1099)

ABOUT THE AUTHOR

Hellooo, I'm Katie, but if you've got to this point in the book, you probably know that already!

I'm a crochet designer based in the seaside town of Hastings, and I work from my colourful home studio – alongside my mum Annie – creating crochet designs that you can craft for yourself.

My aim is to show you how to make fun, colourful hand-crocheted pieces, embracing the practices of an old craft but giving it a new twist. I hope to pass on my passion, as well as the best tips and tricks I have learnt along the way. I have had a crochet brand for the last 10 years. I set it up after graduating from Central Saint Martins, London, after studying Fashion Design: Knit for seven years (yes, I feel that was maybe two years too many, too!).

After graduating, I originally had a fashion line where we made all the pieces in my studio in London, and they were stocked in luxury stores worldwide. As the brand grew, we were exploring how to scale it up, but I started to feel distanced from my pieces; I wanted to keep hand-producing them and have control of the supply chain. I also missed the crafting community that I loved. So, in 2017 I decided to pivot the brand and launch my *Make-It-Yourself Collection*, which puts the task of constructing the garment into the hands of the customer, inviting them to join in with the love of crafting, and making luxury fashion accessible!

My crochet creations have been showcased at the Victoria and Albert Museum as part of its *Fashioned from Nature* exhibition and at the Ferragamo museum in Florence. I have also appeared as a Judge on TV's *Kirstie's Handmade Christmas* and made crochet garments for Paris Fashion Week. A huge career highlight was having my work in one of the main windows of Selfridge's Oxford Street Store in London. But my all-time favourite thing to do is to sit down with a bunch of people who love crochet and to craft together. Please come and join me in my love of colourful craft and enter our world where you can make something amazing for yourself, consciously crafted by you!

KATIE JONES

SUPPLIERS

Support your local yarn stores whenever you can! Here's a rundown of the yarns I used for the project samples:

Shape It Up Blanket
Variations 1 and 2: Hobbii Amigo Chunky

Beret
Variation 1: Hayfield Bonus DK, 2 strands worked at the same time
Variation 2: Hobbii Honey Bunny Candy

Cushion Cover
Variations 1 and 2: Hobbii Amigo XL

Knot Bag
Variation 1: Shiny Happy Cotton, Wool and The Gang
Variation 2: Hobbii Flash It!

Collar
Variation 1: Mixed DK stash, wool and acrylic
Variation 2: Mix of Hobbii Cotton 8/6 and Lovecrafts Paintbox Cotton DK

Perfect Pouch
Variations 1 and 2: Mix of Hobbii Cotton 8/6 and Lovecrafts Paintbox Cotton DK

Neckerchief Scarf
Variation 1: Sirdar Stories Cotton Mix DK
Variation 2: Hobbii Amigo XL

Cozy Cowboy Slipper Socks
Variations 1 and 2: Hobbii Amigo XL

Floor Cushion Cozy
Variations 1 and 2: Hobbii Friends Ribbon

Simple Squares Shopper
Variation 1: Hobbii Honey Bunny
Variation 2: Hobbii Honey Bunny Candy mixed with King Cole Tinsel yarn and King Cole Moments eyelash yarns

Colour Lovin' Coatigan
Variation 1: Hobbii Honey Bunny
Variation 2: Hobbii Cloudy Delight and Hobbii Portabello with 2 strands of Hobbii Diablo

Bonnet
Variation 1: Hobbii Amigo XL
Variation 2: Stylecraft Special DK worked with 1 ply of Hobbii Kid Silk in the same colour

Patchwork Jumper
Variation 1: Hayfield Bonus DK
Variation 2: Sirdar Stories Cotton Blend DK

Tabard
Stitch and Story Lil' Merino

Vest
Variation 1 (vest): Feeling good yarn, Wool and the Gang and Hobbii Friends Merino (2 strands)
Variation 2 (waistcoat): Hobbii Friends Cotton 8/4 and Hobbii Kid Silk, 2 strands worked together

THANKS

A huge, massive thank you to you! Yes, you, dear reader! Thank you for supporting me and reading this book. I hope these projects bring you joy, that I have taught you a nifty trick or tip along the way and that you're inspired to pick up that hook and start crafting something amazing!

A massive thank you to my amazing models who rocked that crochet so well! You were all brilliant – Hannah, Evie, Claudia, Marisa and Ted. Plus, thanks to all those backstage hands and helpers on set: Abigail, Merve, Imogen, Suki, and Phoebe.

To my ride or die, wonderful photographer and bestie, Rachel Manns, thank you for working on this project with me at this big time in your life! And thanks for being my absolute rock through it all; there's no one else I would rather work with. Thank you for being there through it all – LOVE YOU!

To my editor Chelsea, tech editor Lindsay, illustrator Esther and layout legend Claire, thank you for bearing with me and for all your help and patience through this project. Juggling being a new mum and working has been a learning curve and you have all been beyond amazing and supportive. Thank you!

As always, the hugest of thanks to my Mumma, Annie, for the many, many hours crocheting with me, cups of tea, sewing in ends, babysitting and all-round amazingness. I couldn't do any of this without you! Thank you to my husband, Tom, for the constant support, for caring for me and the bab so brilliantly and for putting up with yarn and projects in every spot you can imagine in the house! Love you lots!

A big shout out to Jackie at Hobbii Yarns for so much yarn support. Thank you so much for filling my house with so many brilliant, colourful yarns to use in these projects. Thanks to the lovely team at Sirdar, too!

This book is dedicated to my beautiful bab. It was a bit mad for me to juggle this project and to welcome you to the world, but you will now have many, many mini sweaters made for you using all my leftover yarns. Thank you for being a sweet munchkin and sleeping so I could type! Love you endlessly!

xxxx